UNPLUG YOUR ROBOT

The secret to lasting happiness

KARIN KISER
International bestselling author of
Lighten Your Load

Camino Chronicles Press
9450 Mira Mesa Blvd, Suite 320
San Diego, CA 92126

This book has been registered with the Library of Congress.

ISBN: 978-1-7335759-4-2

Printed in the United States of America

Camino
Chronicles
PRESS

To my Higher Self

Contents

Introduction

Are you fired up in the morning, eager to jump out of bed and embrace the day with enthusiasm? Do you have a regular sense of excitement, satisfaction or joy? Do you feel clear and with purpose or are you wondering right now if those things are even possible?

They are.

Maybe you wake up feeling tired or anxious. Perhaps you get caught up in daily to-dos and obligations and then wonder where the day went. Maybe you've thought a few times, "Is this all there is?" or "Is this really what life is about?"

The answer is no.

Life is about much more—not more stuff and more tasks. No. Life is about more wonder, newness and adventure. More variety, more inspiration—in essence, more *aliveness*.

You can feel enthusiastic and happy on a daily basis. Clarity and balance *are* possible. Not just for some people. For you. You'll need to shake things up a bit though. You'll need to unplug your robot.

What is your robot? I'll give you an example. Have you ever witnessed a couple in a restaurant who seemed completely checked out? They barely look at or speak to each other during the meal. They appear to be going through the motions. Perhaps they were at the same restaurant last week, ordering the same thing from the same waitress.

For most of us, much of our day is run on autopilot. We park the car in front of our house only to realize we have no memory of the drive home. We do things like brushing our teeth or putting on a shirt the same way every time. The same arm goes in first, the same shoelace gets tied first, virtually 100% of the time. We perform these activities unconsciously, all the while our conscious mind chatters at us nonstop.

When our autopilot is on and that robotic mind is running the show, it is impossible to be present in the moment. Instead, we repeatedly rehash the past or react to external events. Our mind urges us to obsessively plan for the future. When the autopilot is on, we're not fully alive. We're cut off from the greater, bigger part of ourselves who is naturally happy, healthy, energetic and peaceful and who lives in harmony with ourself, with others and with nature.

You can add more awareness, synchronicity and exuberance to your life by unplugging your robot. Unfortunately, unplugging the robot—or change of any kind—can be a bit scary. We are comfortable in our routines and habits, even if they are ultimately unsatisfying.

The good news is, change doesn't have to be stressful or scary. In fact, it can be exciting, exhilarating, enlightening and downright fun. In *Unplug Your Robot*, I share my system for creating the life you were meant to live, not the one your parents, your college degree or society thinks you should be living.

People often think unplugging means taking a break from their jobs, obligations and routines and going on vacation. They change the scenery, go to the beach or to the mountains to chill out. Yes, vacations are great. But for most of us, this downtime consists of only a few weeks per year. What about all the other days in between? How are you living those?

This book is about those days. It's about taking that vacation-like sense of relaxation, flow and renewal into your regular life. It's about unplugging your robot and experiencing more freedom, right now.

It's not always the outer circumstances that need to change. It's often how you relate to the external world that could use an upgrade. There is a way to add optimism, joy, wonder and purpose to whatever circumstances you find yourself in. I've done it in my own life and so have my clients. You can too.

In *Unplug Your Robot*, you'll get the roadmap to feel more empowered and excited. It's a guide for living your life to the maximum. You'll discover how to unplug from unconscious routine and live each moment with energy, enthusiasm and clarity.

Sure, you could continue to do the same things in the same way, day in and day out. It's predictable, it's safe and it's comfortable. But it's only half living. Life is not about habits and routines. It's not about waking up at the same time, eating the same breakfast and going to the same job for decades. Life is not about sameness.

Living fully is about creativity, wonder, connection, adventure and utilizing all of your senses. Life is about experiencing more aliveness, however that is defined for you. For some, that might mean selling your business or moving across the country. But it doesn't have to be that dramatic. There's a reason why the subtitle of this book is called The Secret to *Lasting* Happiness. Taking a vacation, doing a digital detox and going on a retreat are all ways to boost your happiness but the effects are usually temporary. The strategies included here offer immediate ways to unplug your robot and feel more alive wherever you are.

In *Unplug Your Robot*, you'll learn how to rediscover your true nature, access more vitality and start living more fully. You'll feel excited and enthusiastic not just about your life, but about your day-to-day as well.

In my previous two books in the Dare to Be Aware™ series, *Lighten Your Load* and *Free and Clear*, I suggested reading through the book once before taking action. Not here. In *Unplug Your Robot*, when you get to an action step, set the book aside and put the strategy into practice right then. Why wait until the end of the book when you can be happy now?

Let's begin.

Part One

YOU'RE PLUGGED IN

CHAPTER ONE

What is the Robot?

So, what is this robot anyway?

The robot is the part of us that goes through the motions, that does the same things in the same order without consciously thinking about it. The robot is also what we absorb from society, the mainstream, the proverbial "they say…". Have you ever wondered who exactly *they* is? It's our collective conditioning, norms we've consciously or unconsciously accepted as true. We get this conditioning from our parents, our schools, our friends. It also comes from Hollywood movies, magazines, the nightly news and television.

By the way, there's a reason it's called a TV *program*. When we watch a television program, we are the ones being programmed, whether we realize it or not. Our subconscious mind absorbs it all, everything we see, everything we hear. The constant stimulation from the screen puts us in a hypnotic state. You've seen it. Try to get the attention of a small child engrossed in a television program and it's like they're in a trance. That's the robot.

The robot includes beliefs and attitudes we pick up from advertising. There are paid-for product placements in films that encourage us to associate them with the popular actors or characters in the film. Commercials are cleverly crafted to get us to compare ourselves to and compete with others. Mainstream media contribute to turning us into a consumption robot by making us feel inadequate.

The robot is not just the media and entertainment industries, however. Our political, economic, education and health care systems, while perhaps originally designed to provide more individual liberties, have since been co-opted into state dependency machines. We now have big pharma, a state schooling system, a disease management system, industrial agriculture and energy infrastructure that keep us plugged in and dependent. It works. The robot in us engages in mindless, unconscious consumption. It is externally focused, overstimulated and an active seeker of acceptance, approval and praise from others. It leaves us distracted, disconnected and disempowered. And we continue to go along with it.

It wasn't always this way.

Think back to when you were a small child. Do you remember how you used to feel? Every day was a new adventure waiting to be explored. You loved trying new things. You were full of wonder and creativity. You possessed seemingly unlimited energy. You wanted to skip, cause mischief, ask endless questions and explore your surroundings.

You are still that kid, but since then you have likely experienced decades of not feeling so open or welcoming of change. The excitement is still there, however, deep under the layers of frustration, disappointment and daily minutiae you have piled on top. The daily minutiae and disappointment are part of your robot. The robot is not you. The child eager to wake up and experience a new day of adventure is still inside you. *That* is your true nature.

The problem is that as we grow older, we lose that palpable sense of awe, enthusiasm and curiosity. By the time we reach grade school, we have been told "no" hundreds or thousands of times. Perhaps our natural inquisitive, adventurous and expressive nature was not always encouraged by our parents and teachers. So over time, we learned to stop asking so many questions.

Now is the time to start asking questions again.

What is the robot? It's the external influences and programming, including our own self-sabotaging thoughts and beliefs, that want to keep us small, safe and secure. Luckily, we can unplug it. But first, see how much of your life is run by the robot in you. In the next chapter, you'll take a quick self-test to find out.

CHAPTER TWO

The Self-Test. How Much of the Robot is Running You?

How much of you is plugged into the robot? Take this 30-question quiz to find out. Grab a pen and paper, number it 1 to 30 and leave space to jot down your answers—A, B, C, D or E—next to each number.

---

1. When you put on your shoes and socks, do you always start with the same foot?

    A. No
    B. Yes
    C. Don't know

If you answered "don't know," find out by putting on your socks and shoes right now. Notice how you do it.

2. How much television do you typically watch in a day? By television, I am referring to anything coming through your television or computer screen, such as Netflix, news or entertainment programming.

    A. Less than an hour
    B. 1-2 hours
    C. 3+ hours

3. When was the last time you tried a new restaurant?

    A. More than a month ago
    B. This week
    C. Within the last month

4. How often do you say things like, "That's just the way it is" or "There's nothing I can do about it?"

    A. Occasionally

    B. A lot

    C. Never

5. Have you gone on vacation to the same city and stayed at the same hotel more than twice?

    A. No

    B. Yes

6. How often do you experience boredom?

    A. Every day

    B. Most days

    C. Occasionally

    D. Rarely

    E. Never

7. How much time do you spend per day using digital devices such as your phone, tablet and computer to check email, engage in social media and Google stuff? (While at work counts too.)

    A. Less than one hour per day

    B. 2-3 hours

    C. 4-6 hours

    D. More than 6 hours

8. Think about what you ate for breakfast today. Did you eat the same thing for breakfast yesterday as well?

    A. Yes

    B. No

9. Have you been eating the same thing for breakfast for the last week?

    A. Yes

    B. No

10. The last month?

    A. Yes

    B. No

11. Do you regularly choose your clothes or grooming practices based on how they will appear to others?

    A. No

    B. Sometimes

    C. Yes

12. If a new friend were to show up at your house in an old car with faded paint and rust spots, would you feel embarrassed to be seen in it?

    A. Yes

    B. No

    C. Depends on where we are going

13. How often do you think what your friends, neighbors or coworkers have is better than what you have?

    A. Occasionally

    B. All the time

    C. Rarely

14. Do you regularly tell stories from your high school or college years?

    A. Yes

    B. No

15. When was the last time you engaged in a random act of kindness or initiated an in-person conversation with a stranger?

    A. I can't remember

    B. Last month

    C. Last week

    D. Yesterday

    E. Today

16. Quickly jot down five things you often say you'd like to do or experience someday.

    1.

    2.

    3.

    4.

    5.

What's the likelihood of your actually experiencing one of those things in the next four months?

    A. 75-100%
    B. 51-74%
    C. 26-50%
    D. 0-25%

17. List seven of the happiest or most fun moments in your life thus far.

    1.

    2.

    3.

    4.

    5.

    6.

    7.

How long did it take you to answer that last question?

    A. Less than 30 seconds

    B. 30-60 seconds

    C. 1-5 minutes

    D. I still haven't thought of 7 things

18. How many of the moments you listed above occurred within the last 18 months?

    A. 0

    B. 1

    C. More than one

19. How frequently do you experience anxiety, fear or worry about the future?

    A. Every day

    B. Most days

    C. Occasionally

    D. Rarely

    E. Never

20. When you imagine your retirement years, which of the following best describes how you would like to experience them?

    A. Comfortable and content

    B. Secure and stable

    C. Adventurous and vibrant

    D. Much the same as my current day-to-day

21. Do you wake up at the same time every morning?

    A. Yes

    B. Usually

    C. No

22. When someone criticizes or insults you, you typically

    A. Take it personally and feel hurt
    B. Brush it off and assume that person is having a bad day
    C. Get upset or angry

23. Do you believe there is a specific purpose to your life?

    A. Yes
    B. No

24. How soon upon waking do you check your phone?

    A. Within the first 5 minutes
    B. Approximately 15-30 minutes after waking up
    C. About an hour after getting out of bed
    D. More than an hour after

25. When was the last time you laughed out loud for longer than 10 seconds?

    A. Yesterday
    B. Today
    C. This week
    D. Can't remember

26. How often do you have the television or radio on for background noise when you are not actively watching or listening to it?

    A. Most days
    B. Every day
    C. Occasionally
    D. Rarely
    E. Never

27. Do you keep your cell phone turned on overnight while you
    are sleeping (even if only for the alarm function)?

    A. Yes, always
    B. Most of the time
    C. Rarely
    D. Never

28. When was the last time you went outside just to spend
    time outdoors?

    A. Last weekend
    B. Yesterday
    C. I don't remember
    D. A month or two ago

29. Do you often criticize, find fault or judge other people, either
    out loud or silently to yourself?

    A. Yes, all the time
    B. No
    C. Sometimes

30. Put on your socks and shoes again and notice how you do it. Did
    you start with the same foot as you did earlier for question #1?

    A. Yes
    B. No
    C. Not sure

SCORESHEET

Time to add up your points and see how you did.

1. A = 3 points
    B = 4 points
    C = 1 point

2. A = 2 points
    B = 4 points
    C = 7 points

3. A = 3 points
    B = 0 points
    C = 1 point

4. A = 3 points
    B = 5 points
    C = 1 point

5. A = 0 points
    B = 3 points

6. A = 6 points
    B = 5 points
    C = 3 points
    D = 1 point
    E = 0 points

7. A = 1 point
    B = 2 points
    C = 5 points
    D = 7 points

8. A = 2 points
    B = 1 point

9. A = 3 points
    B = 1 point

10. A = 4 points
    B = 1 point

11. A = 1 point
    B = 3 points
    C = 4 points

12. A = 4 points
    B = 1 point
    C = 5 points

13. A = 3 points
    B = 5 points
    C = 1 point

14. A = 4 points
    B = 0 points

15. A = 6 points
    B = 5 points
    C = 3 points
    D = 1 point
    E = 0 points

16. A = 0 points
    B = 3 points
    C = 5 points
    D = 7 points

17. A = 0 points
    B = 1 point
    C = 2 points
    D = 6 points

18. A = 5 points
    B = 2 points
    C = 0 points

19. A = 7 points
    B = 5 points
    C = 2 points
    D = 1 point
    E = 0 points

20. A = 3 points
    B = 5 points
    C = 1 point
    D = 3 points

21. A = 3 points
    B = 2 points
    C = 1 point

22. A = 5 points
    B = 0 points
    C = 5 points

23. A = 1 point
    B = 6 points

24. A = 7 points
    B = 5 points
    C = 3 points
    D = 1 point

25. A = 1 point
    B = 0 points
    C = 1 point
    D = 5 points

26. A = 5 points
    B = 6 points
    C = 3 points
    D = 1 point
    E = 0 points

27. A = 6 points
    B = 5 points
    C = 2 points
    D = 0 points

28. A = 1 point
    B = 0 points
    C = 7 points
    D = 4 points

29. A = 5 points
    B = 1 point
    C = 3 points

30. A = 2 points
    B = 0 points
    C = 1 point

IS THE ROBOT RUNNING YOU?

Regardless of your score, the short answer is yes. It's a matter of degree. Your score indicates the degree to which you are currently plugged in. Take a look:

Your robot is plugged in and has completely taken over
(115 to 150 points)

Unfortunately, bigger points here indicates a bigger robot! Don't despair, this high score simply means you will have lots of options for unplugging it. Read on.

Live-in robot
(83 to 114 points)

Your robot might have been just a visitor before, but now it has taken up residence and is eyeing the master suite. In other words, your robot isn't in total control yet, but it's close. You've come to the right place.

Part-time robot
(51 to 82)

Not bad. With a few upgrades, you can turn off the autopilot and be the full-time driver in your life.

Toy robot
(17 to 50)

You are aware of the robot and you know that the robot is not you. Well done. The good news is that no matter how small your robot currently is, it is still plugged in to the outlet. In the chapters ahead, I'll show you how to unplug it.

CHAPTER THREE

Dare to Be Aware.™ We're Plugged In and We Don't Even Know It

Here's something I didn't mention about the quiz in the last chapter. Even if you scored relatively well, the robot in you still might be large and in charge. Why is this? The robot in us loves quizzes and is quite good at taking them. It makes sense, doesn't it? We have years of experience with quizzes and all things multiple-choice, stemming back to our childhood and more than a decade in school.

Rather than an assessment of how much the robot is running you, the quiz serves as a gauge of how aware you are that it is running you, at least to some degree. It's our robot that jumps in with the immediate "yes" or "no" answer without thinking about it. The robot enjoys trying to outsmart things and thrives on external validation, scoring well or at least doing better than others. Therefore, the "I don't know" or "can't remember" answers could indicate fewer robotic tendencies than the quick "yes" or "no" answers from the mind.

Now, consider this: About 80% of your thoughts are the same thoughts you had yesterday. And that's not all. The bulk of those thoughts are likely negative. Closely monitor your thoughts for a day or two and you'll experience it firsthand. Our mind gives us an ongoing commentary, 24 hours a day. The mind is that robotic voice in your head that has a running conversation about nothing in particular, nonstop, 24/7. It's a thought-machine that, left to its own devices, constantly tells us what we should and shouldn't believe and what we should and shouldn't do. Some refer to this as the ego or the personality. I call it *The Should.*

Another part of the robot is our subconscious mind that operates behind the scenes yet controls 95% of our day. It allows us to do routine activities like brushing our teeth, putting on clothes and driving the car without having to re-learn how to do those activities each time. If you drive to work, chances are good you take the same route every day. You've done it hundreds of times. It's become natural, almost effortless. So, in essence, the robot is driving the car, not you. Your attention is wandering around, engrossed in thought—those same thoughts you had yesterday.

You might think this mind wandering is a good thing, that multitasking is useful and makes you more productive. After all, you can drive the car and simultaneously plan out your day at work. But the real you is asleep at the wheel. We don't realize we are plugged into the robot because so much of what we view as normal is, in fact, a symptom of being plugged in. Common symptoms that our robot is in control include:

- Comparing ourselves to others
- Placing great importance on consistency and predictability, especially in other people
- Seeking approval from others, fishing for compliments and desiring other forms of external validation
- Frequently pondering or rehashing the past
- Believing there is not enough time in the day
- Finding comfort in being busy
- Feeling frequent anxiety, fear or worry about the future
- Doing something we're expected to do when there is no longer any joy in it

- Experiencing comfort in our routines, where our days are more or less the same
- Believing more is better
- Thinking our circumstances are to blame for not being as happy, fit or wealthy as we could be
- Getting easily offended and taking things personally

The robot in us thinks all of the above are a normal part of life. It's not normal. It's not how things are supposed to be. The secret to lasting happiness is to realize you're plugged into the robot and that you have the power to unplug yourself from it.

The robot consists of more than the thought-machine and the autopilot I mentioned earlier. It also includes conditioning we get from our family, school and religion during our formative years, typically before the age of seven. Regardless of what type of childhood you experienced, you picked up thoughts, beliefs and behaviors from your immediate environment that you would not necessarily have chosen for yourself had you been aware of all the alternatives. Our family, friends and caregivers imprint on us and, in the early years, that is all we know. There is nothing wrong in this.

As we develop into our adolescent and young adult years, that circle of influence expands to encompass what I call The Machine. Otherwise known as mainstream society, The Machine includes the norms, traditions and beliefs we take on from the collective. In the West, it could be the assumption that the path to success is to work hard, go to college, get a good job and make a lot of money, which is then reinforced by the movies we watch and advertising we're exposed to. Those beliefs and assumptions become part of our robot as well.

Our cultural mythology also forms part of The Machine, and its assumptions are rarely called into question. Assumptions that we need people to rule over us and tell us what to do, whether in the form of government, the church or the courts. Or the assumption that human nature is inherently bad or flawed and, therefore, we need others to fix and guide us.

In essence, the robot is the sum total of the Not You—all that has been placed on you or unconsciously adopted by you since you were a young child. In contrast, the real you is the innate essence you came into the world with. This book will help you to wake up from the collective trance, find your center and live consciously with purpose and joy.

PART TWO

PULL THE PLUG

CHAPTER FOUR

Grab the Plug

"Events don't determine whether or not you're going to be happy. You determine whether or not you're going to be happy."

MICHAEL SINGER

As we saw in the last chapter and in the quiz, to unplug the robot we must first realize we're plugged in, at least to some degree. The next step is believing you have the power to unplug the robot and get into the driver's seat of your life. Only you can do it. You are responsible. Being responsible is not the same thing as being to blame. Being responsible is just that: Response able. Able to respond.

While you may not have been consciously aware that the robot was slowly assuming control over time, now that you *are* aware, you have the power to change it.

The truth is, we are much more powerful than we give ourselves credit for. Even in the face of obstacles, money issues, health challenges, family or relationship dynamics, you can choose how you feel about it all.

> *"You can choose the thought that makes you worry or the thought that makes you happy; the things that thrill you, or the things that worry you. You have the choice in every moment."*
> **ABRAHAM-HICKS**

You create the world you live in. You create it with the thoughts you think, the food you eat, the stories you tell, the habits you hold, as well as the people and things you surround yourself with. What are you currently creating? Look around you. You had a hand in creating everything you perceive.

We can choose what we do and how we think. No one can make us feel anything. That bears repeating. *No one can make us feel anything.* Statements such as "She made me mad" or "That made me late" are false. Our thoughts, feelings and reactions are a moment-by-moment decision. We can choose to be happy, regardless of what's going on around us. We can create any thought, feeling or state of being at will. Don't think so? Try this: Think of an incident in your life when you felt betrayed or hurt by someone close to you. In your mind's eye, take yourself back to that time. Replay the incident in vivid detail. What the person said or did. How sad, lonely or hurt you felt. Feel those emotions for the next minute or two.

Observe your current mental and emotional state. If you're like most people, your mood is now different, perhaps more pessimistic, sad or angry than before you did the exercise. That's how powerful you are. You can change your mood with as little as 60 seconds of pondering. Incredible!

Let's return to a more positive state of mind, shall we? Bring to mind one of the happiest moments in your life when things were really in the flow. Where were you? Who else was there? Replay in your mind's eye the details of what made that moment or event so special. Feel it in your body as though it were happening again now. Recall the sights, the smells, the sounds, the sensations. Feel the gratitude, the love, the awe or the excitement for a few moments. Notice how you have again altered your mood—perhaps dramatically—from a few moments ago.

> *"You are not your thoughts and feelings and you do not have to believe them, react to them or be driven or tyrannized by them."*
>
> **JON KABAT-ZINN, AUTHOR OF** *FULL CATASTROPHE LIVING*

We are in charge. When plugged into the robot, we tend to think stress, anxiety, boredom, worry, happiness, fulfillment or peace are caused by external things like our family, job, spouse, government, economy or the weather. Not true. Our state of being, whether positive or negative, comes from our reaction to things and the meaning we give them. The reaction and the meaning are supplied by us. This can be tough to acknowledge because doing so means admitting we can no longer blame anyone or anything. We are creating it all. When we're plugged in, we don't realize we're creating our reality. When we unplug the robot, we get into the driver's seat of our life. We become conscious creators — responsible, deliberate, free.

Unplugging your robot doesn't mean you'll never have an off day, feel sad or get angry. The difference is that you are more aware when those things happen. With greater awareness, you can reframe and redirect those less-than-awesome moments and use them as opportunities to actively choose the reality you prefer. You are in charge.

Now that you know you're in the driver's seat, the next chapters will describe where you can go. Fasten your seatbelt!

CHAPTER FIVE

Unplug from the Past

"Living in the past is equivalent to living in a psychic cemetery where you confer with problematic corpses on a regular basis."

CAROLINE MYSS

Once you recognize you have the power to modify your mood and change your reality for the better, the next step is to make room in your life for more happiness, excitement and fulfillment. Take a moment to observe your surroundings. Look at the physical environment in your home, your office or your car. Is it spacious and inviting? Does that space promote a feeling of relaxation and ease or does all of your physical stuff make you tense and weary?

The physical clutter that we see outside of us is a mirror of the clutter we have inside. We often unconsciously generate clutter to distract us. Clutter keeps us externally focused. That focus on all things outside of us and our tendency toward distraction are part of the robot. The robot blocks us from realizing that the source of all that clutter and physical disorder is internal.

Ever wonder why the effects of decluttering your home, cleaning out your car or paring down your wardrobe are rarely permanent? The robot within us is eternally dissatisfied and addicted to more. The robot loves busyness and stuff. Physical stuff keeps us managing, arranging, storing, cleaning, repairing, lots of "ing." All that do-ing serves as a form of distraction, which then clutters our mental space as well.

MAKE SPACE

Let's create some physical and mental space today. Look around you again and identify one thing you are no longer using or that doesn't positively contribute to your life. Set it aside to recycle, donate or give to someone else. Better yet, put that item in your car. Do this now, rather than adding it to your to-do list for later.

Feels good, doesn't it?

Now consider your digital environment — the unread emails waiting in your inbox, your saved emails, computer files, phone contacts, apps, text threads.... Are you beginning to feel anxious just reading that? Digital clutter also takes a physical and mental toll.

Let's experience another quick win in creating space. Go to your email inbox and identify five messages you can permanently delete right now. Prime candidates include emails from shopping sites and newsletters you tell yourself you might read later. Delete five of them now. If you have unread emails from more than six months ago, challenge yourself to delete them immediately. Your mind might scream, "But what if they are important, what if I might need them?" If that were really true, you would have read them by now. Either way, that person or company will email you again soon, so there is little danger of deleting anything really significant.

Making space is critical for having more of what you really want in life. It goes beyond decluttering. Creating meaningful space means getting to the root of why you accumulate and hold on to physical, mental and digital stuff. Breaking the declutter-reclutter habit in our consumption-obsessed culture is so important that I wrote an entire book about it. You can download free bonus chapters from my book *Free and Clear: 7 Steps to Declutter Your Home and Your Head* at www.KarinKiser.com/free-and-clear/.

Set aside a block of time this week to calmly reduce your digital clutter. Determine what else in your home or office could be cleaned up or cleared out. When you unplug from some of your physical and digital stuff (we'll get to the mental stuff in Chapter Eight), you loosen the grip of your robot and create space for your inner peace and calm to emerge.

UNPLUG FROM YOUR STORY

Unplugging from the past is not confined to our physical stuff and old computer files. It also means disengaging from the stories we tell over and over.

The robot in us is filled with stories. There's the story of why you moved to the city you currently live in. You have a story of how and why a relationship ended. There's a story behind virtually every belief or opinion you hold. We tell these stories repeatedly either out loud to others or silently to ourselves. Unfortunately, the more we relay a story, the more attached to it we become. We start to identify with it, reinforcing our own self-programming with each recounting.

> *"Frequently we do not leave the past behind. We clasp on to it. We dissect it, and let fears for the future, tempered by the past, unconsciously prevent us from taking up the task eternal."*
>
> **RAY SIMPSON, AUTHOR OF *EXPLORING CELTIC SPIRITUALITY***

Our robot operates through the filters of our past. We use the past to model future outcomes, which is why many of the outcomes tend to repeat in our lives even if they are undesirable. Truth be told, the past is only valuable in that it got you here. The details are largely irrelevant to your present moment. Yet the robot in us keeps us anchored in the past and attached to our stories, the burden of which becomes heavier as time goes by. We've been trained to focus on the negative and have spent years, perhaps decades, retelling the same disempowering stories.

The following exercise will set the framework to unplug from your old stories so you can create a new one full of possibility. That new story will be true to who you are at the core rather than who you currently think you are based on your past.

EXERCISE: MY STORY OF THE PAST

You will begin this exercise by writing down the significant events in your life—negative or positive—that have shaped you as a person, starting with your earliest memory. Warning: This exercise can take a while but the process itself is quite transformational. It allows you to see valuable patterns and themes in your life. Once you see the patterns and habits that do not contribute to your happiness, you have the power to change them.

Don't worry, you do not need to write a 200-page autobiography. The purpose of this life review is to highlight what you consider to be important events. There's no wrong way to do the exercise. Some people start from childhood and do a single chronology. Others find it more useful to divide their life into segments according to major topics, such as:

- Relationship with your family growing up
- Your school years
- Jobs and career
- Personal relationships: boyfriends, girlfriends, spouses
- Discovering your passions or natural talents
- Obstacles you've overcome
- Happiest moments and major successes
- Roles and labels you have adopted: mother, daughter, employee/employer, conservative/liberal
- Major lessons learned
- Accidents, injuries or trauma
- Your strengths and weaknesses
- How others would describe you

For best results, avoid listing events in your life like an impersonal timeline, such as: "My parents divorced when I was 9. We moved into an apartment with my mom when I was 12. Had a serious car accident at 17." If an incident is significant enough to mention, it is important to write about *why* it is meaningful, *how* you felt about it at the time and how you feel about it *now*.

Really go for it. Write it all down as if you were telling your stories one last and final time. No one will read it but you, so no holding back. Put the book down now and get started.

It's quite possible that the robot in you is telling you not to do this exercise. "Just keep reading," it may say. "You can come back to this later." Resist the urge to put it off until you "have more time" or "after you finish X, Y or Z." That's the robot talking.

Start to notice the stories you tell over and over. Perhaps "you can do it later" is a recurring theme in your life. Pick one of the segments above (relationship with family, career, happiest moments) and quickly jot down whatever comes to mind. The process of transferring parts of your story from your head to the paper or keyboard is strangely liberating and creates some much-needed space in your mind and body.

Become the detective in your own life. Look for patterns and themes. When pondering the jobs you've had over the years, for instance, perhaps you notice some similar traits in the bosses you've had. Or, as you think about your friendships and intimate relationships, maybe there's a common thread in how they have ended. Perhaps you notice something about yourself or a way of being that was common to each of those experiences. Highlight any common threads or themes.

As you work with the material in *Unplug Your Robot* in the coming days, keep your detective hat on. Notice the stories you tell others, as well as the ones you tell yourself with your mental dialog. When you notice one, add it to your My Story of The Past.

.

CHAPTER SIX

Unplug from Conditioning

Hopefully by now you've spent some time with the My Story of The Past exercise and you have written about the meaningful events from your early years. As you'll see in this chapter, we receive the bulk of our conditioning as children. No matter how great your childhood, you downloaded a variety of programs in your first seven years of life. We all did. There is no avoiding it. Before our conscious mind develops, we take everything in, unquestioned and unfiltered, by observing the behavior of those around us.

What is this conditioning? It's the way we perceive ourselves and our surroundings. It is a function of what is silently modeled and audibly taught to us by our parents, siblings, teachers, friends, relatives and religions. As part of this indoctrination, we take in everything, including disempowering and self-sabotaging beliefs.

Yes, I said indoctrination. Indoctrination is simply the process of teaching a person to accept a set of beliefs uncritically. It's a trigger word for some but it doesn't necessarily imply that malicious intent is involved. Indoctrination and conditioning include everything we observe, absorb and learn before we are old enough to question it and before our conscious mind fully develops. Everything we have ever seen, thought, heard, felt or experienced is stored in our subconscious mind.

> *"The chief cause of human errors is to be found in the prejudices picked up in childhood."*
> RENÉ DESCARTES

Many of us are conditioned to believe in Santa Claus, Heaven or Evil. Nothing wrong in that, of course, but it doesn't stop there. Think back to some of the phrases you heard your parents say repeatedly. They offer clues to the attitudes and beliefs prevalent in your early environment. That environment influenced what you believe now. Consider whether any of these rings a bell:

Phrase	Underlying Programming
Money doesn't grow on trees.	Scarcity
You better be a good boy.	Obedience
No pain, no gain.	Struggle; normalized suffering
That's just the way it is.	Powerlessness; helplessness
Because I said so.	Authority
People don't change.	Victimhood; pessimism
Better safe than sorry.	Fear
We can't afford it.	Scarcity
You have to work hard to…	Struggle as normalized and praiseworthy
Give them an inch and they'll take a mile.	Distrust
You will understand when you get older.	Inadequacy

There are countless others that, upon further examination with our conscious mind, may not be true at all.

At about the age of seven our conscious mind develops. However, as we saw in Chapter Three, only 5% of our day is run by our conscious mind. According to stem cell biologist and author Bruce Lipton, the other 95% of our day is run by our subconscious programming, i.e., the robot, that has automatically absorbed everything in our environment from day one.

The school system plays a pivotal role in molding and polishing our robot. It is no coincidence that as our conscious mind begins to come on board, we are sent to schools to be "educated." How are we educated? Indoors, seated at a desk for hours at a time, memorizing facts and figures for more than a decade.

The mandatory government education system in the United States was modeled on the Prussian system at a time when good workers and soldiers were needed, and by good, I mean obedient. It hasn't changed much since. We're educated to be employees, soldiers and above all, consumers. You might be thinking, "Well, I went to public school and never worked in a factory or became a soldier." I didn't either. Yet the system teaches us to obey authority figures and seek external approval nonetheless.

> *"Schools are to establish fixed habits of response to authority. That's why it takes 12 years. You're to respond reflexively to anyone in a position of authority who tells you what to do."*
>
> **JOHN TAYLOR GATTO, NEW YORK STATE TEACHER OF THE YEAR**
> **AND AUTHOR OF *DUMBING US DOWN***

Government schooling is not set up to nurture each child's individual brilliance. The system values the rational, linear mind at the expense of the creative, intuitive mind. We typically don't come out of that system having discovered joy and a love of life. Instead, we've learned to seek approval from teachers and crave acceptance from other kids. We're taught to compare, compete and comply.

> *"When we become aware of how the school system is a conditioning agent to instill in children obedience to authority, passivity and tolerance to tedium for the sake of external rewards, we begin to question school performance as a metric of well-being. Maybe a healthy child is one who resists schooling and standardization, not one who excels at it."*
>
> CHARLES EISENSTEIN, AUTHOR OF *THE MORE BEAUTIFUL WORLD OUR HEARTS KNOW IS POSSIBLE*

The school system teaches us that from Monday to Friday we must do what we're told and that the evenings and weekends are for freedom — after completing our homework, of course. This conditioning is later reinforced when we become employees, working our way up the ranks, paying our dues and taking our work home with us in hopes of earning something better later.

In my case, I accepted the "work hard, get good grades, go to college and get a good job" assumption. My conditioning supported this as the best path to follow. Implied in that assumption was that happiness was possible when I got the good job and the money that came with it. Happiness was linked with money. Money was linked with working hard. Working hard meant doing things that were tedious, repetitive and time-consuming. None of that turned out to be true.

Recall your childhood years in school and your early years as an employee. How have those years shaped you as a person? What were some of your unquestioned assumptions? Add any memories or impressions that are resurfacing now to your My Story of the Past.

> *"Good education = good job, good money, good things. This has become the universal national banner, hoisted by Harvards as well as high schools. This prescription makes both parent and student easier to regulate and intimidate as long as the connection goes unchallenged either for its veracity or in its philosophical truth."*
>
> JOHN TAYLOR GATTO

As children, we were constantly told what to do and what not to do by our parents and teachers. Our doing or not doing had some very real consequences: various forms of punishment or reward, approval or disapproval, expressions of love or withholding love, validation that we are good or bad. Later on, teachers and parents were replaced by employers telling us what to do. Now government and the media constantly tell us what to think, how to behave and what to buy.

Because of this relentless conditioning, it's no wonder that we actually *want* to be told what to do. Let me say that again. We actually want to be told what to do, at least on some level. I am no exception. Realizing this was a big eye-opener. I had prided myself on being an independent thinker, a rebel even. I regularly questioned things. Nobody likes being told what to do, right? On the surface, we may not like it, but we are conditioned to want it. Why? Because it is easier. Being told what to do releases you of personal responsibility. Let someone else decide. Let someone else take care of it. It's easier to simply go along with what everyone else seems to be doing. Following the rules, however illogical, illegitimate or immoral, is easier than questioning or defying them.

It can feel unsafe to question the powers that be, particularly when we've been trained to seek approval and direction from others. While seeking direction from our family and friends is a natural part of childhood, it becomes a problem when we don't outgrow the need for external validation and instead, carry it around with us the rest of our lives.

Did you ever hear this one as a kid: "If everyone jumped off a bridge, would you too?" Wise words. While we likely answered no (or said nothing at all), if we look around at our world now, we all seem to be jumping off the bridge together, and either denying that it's a bridge or being unaware that we are jumping. As adults, we often cite popular opinion as a reason for our actions, however senseless or destructive.

Rather than consult our own internal guidance, we regularly outsource our authority and decision-making to others, often without realizing it is happening. Our logical mind tells us it makes sense to defer to the experts. After all, as individuals, we can't possibly know enough about the intricacies of the human body, the legal system or the problems of the world to make informed decisions. Better let other individuals—the experts—handle those things.

It is easier to outsource our decision-making than it is to do the research and critical thinking necessary to make informed choices. The mainstream and those in perceived positions of authority know this. They actively participate in our current age of disinformation, where it has become increasingly difficult to distinguish fake news from legitimate sources of credible information. The result? The wedge of doubt is driven further into our ability to be self-referencing and know how to take care of ourselves.

Take your power and agency back. Reclaim your inner authority and plug into *that* rather than continue to mechanically yield to outside influences. Start to question the previously unquestionable. What if a lot of what you were taught to believe is wrong? That is one of our fundamental fears. Also called cognitive dissonance, it suggests that we would rather hold on to a belief, even if false, than call into question something we've believed all of our lives, which then brings everything about ourselves and our world into doubt.

> *"The universe will validate every belief you hold about the nature of reality."*
> **ALBERTO VILLOLDO**

What if people are inherently good and generous? What if we would prosper without governments that determine how to spend our money? What if we would thrive without insurance companies deciding how much our life is worth and which medical procedures we can receive? What if our lifestyle choices influenced our state of health and wellness far more than the genetic blueprint we came in with? What if doing more isn't the path to happiness? What if, instead of dominating nature and considering it an asset, we were meant to be Earth stewards and caretakers of all life? What if environmental destruction, species extinction and war are a direct result of our getting it wrong?

Uncomfortable, isn't it? The robot in us does not like this discomfort.

A byproduct of the schooling system is our tendency to place undue importance on being consistent and predictable. Because we are taught to value safety and comfort, our default is to remain in our comfort zone.

Are you willing to be wrong? We're conditioned that it's important to be right. Otherwise, you won't get good grades, which means you might not go to college, which means you likely won't get a good job, which means you will have failed at life. Ironically, this fear of being wrong can be cleared by facing it head on, by asking more questions and by examining your beliefs and assumptions with childlike curiosity. Let's do that now.

START ASKING WHY

> *"It is interesting how few questions we actually ask about very everyday things."*
> **DAVID ICKE**

Kids constantly ask why. If you have children, you know this firsthand. If you don't, think back to your own early years. As kids we asked why about everything, often exasperating our parents in the process. For whatever answer they gave, our response was another why. Why? Because the world seemed like such a big, mysterious place with endless things to learn and explore. It still is.

One of the keys to unplugging your robot is to bring some of that curiosity back into your daily life. Start asking why. Act like a detective. Pay attention to what you do and why. Regularly question things, especially your assumptions and beliefs. Here are some questions to get you started:

- Why do I part my hair on this side?
- Why do I drive this way to work?
- Why do I assume my coworker is unfriendly?
- Why do I believe it won't work out?

If you answered "because I always drive this way," "cause it's easy," "I'm used to it" or "it's comfortable," Red Alert! Those are signs of being plugged into the robot. The robot likes control, comfort and routine. "But wait," you might be thinking, "I've driven several routes to work and now I take the same route every day because it's the shortest." Ah, but what if there's a route you haven't yet discovered, that's 5-10 minutes longer but is much more scenic, has fewer cars and leaves you feeling calmer and more relaxed when you arrive?

There's tremendous value in questioning why you do things. Is it out of pure joy, out of obligation or out of simple habit? I make it a practice to regularly question my thoughts, beliefs and actions. In fact, years ago I did an experiment, starting with my breakfast. My internal dialog went something like this:

Me: "Why do I eat a hard-boiled egg in the morning?"

Robot: "It's quick, it's easy and you need protein."

Me: "Is all of that really true?"

Robot: "Yes."

Me: "Really? I'm going to look into this further."

Robot: "Don't bother. Stick with what you know."

Me: "I'm going to investigate. First point: Is it quick? Yes. Yet there are other things equally as quick. Why do I need a quick breakfast anyway? Wouldn't a slower one be more enjoyable? Maybe I will get up a bit earlier to enjoy a slower breakfast."

Me: "Second point: Is it easy? Yes, but only if I take the time to boil the eggs in advance. Truth be told, I have forgotten about the eggs boiling on the stove more than once. Given the advance planning and my forgetfulness in the boiling eggs department, they are not, in fact, easy for me (especially when I factor in the exploded egg cleanup)."

Me: "Third point: I need protein. After researching this point, it turns out that, a) I don't need as much protein as I thought and b) eggs are not the cleanest, highest quality source of protein anyway."

During this detective-like dialog with myself I uncovered a fourth point: "Do I enjoy the egg? No. I never wake up excited to chow down on a hard-boiled egg. That does it. Case closed!"

You can engage in a similar dialog process with your daily habits. For instance, perhaps you decided years ago that your morning routine was the quickest and most efficient way to start the day. But is that still true now? You are not the same person you were yesterday, to say nothing of two months or two years ago. Maybe there's a better way that is more in alignment with your goals, values and life situation now.

> *"If you have always done it that way, it is probably wrong."*
> **CHARLES F. KETTERING**

Question what you have taken for granted and how you think things work. Be open with the wonder and curiosity of a child. Instead of thinking in terms of right and wrong, success and failure, you can choose to think in terms of curiosity and change. Be willing to change your mind based on new information. Dare to interrupt your patterns.

INTERRUPT THE PATTERN

> *"Repetition makes life stale. It brings boredom, indifference and fatigue. If you keep repeating the things you have no real interest in, you grow numb."*
> **DEEPAK CHOPRA**

Routine, which is another characteristic of the robot, allows us to go through life without thinking or questioning things too much. When you activate your imagination and change the way you perform routine activities, you loosen the control of the autopilot that mechanizes your day. You use more of your senses. You become more alive. That aliveness doesn't come from the activity itself. *You* bring the joy, excitement and exuberance *into* the activity. The first step is choosing to believe this is true. The second step is actively applying it in your life.

"If you think adventure is dangerous, try routine, it's lethal."
PAULO COELHO

There's nothing wrong with routine if you engage in each activity consciously, with full awareness. How can you be more present and alive in what you do? Mix it up. If you listen to music while you drive, try driving in silence. If you always put your pants on starting with the right leg, try it for a week with the left leg first. If you normally check email and texts the minute you wake up, experiment with stretching or meditating before you activate your digital devices.

Here are other suggestions to interrupt some of your automatic patterns while simultaneously boosting your awareness:

- Get up an hour earlier or later for no particular reason.
- Use your non-dominant hand for everything: brushing your teeth, opening doors and eating. This is a tough one, so much so that you might need to tie together the fingers of your dominant hand to remind you to use the other one.
- Try something you've never eaten for breakfast.
- Wear something outrageous and see if anyone notices. It doesn't matter whether anyone notices. Either way you will be on high alert and *you* will notice more, both externally in your environment and internally in the way you think and feel.
- Hand-wash your dishes in slow motion and with full attention, as if you were doing it for the very first time.
- Walk for 20 minutes at half the speed you normally walk and pay attention to your surroundings.
- Laugh for no reason.
- Experience a cuisine that is new to you, such as Ethiopian, Russian, Korean or Thai.

- Sleep on the other side of the bed or, better yet, with your head at the other end where your feet normally are.

- If you wake up in the middle of the night and are seemingly wide awake, rather than fret about it, get up and do something that does not involve digital devices, such as stretching or stargazing.

Some of these suggestions may seem silly, but that's the whole point. The robot within us is serious, very serious indeed. You loosen its grip by tapping into your innate silliness and playfulness.

> *"A mind that is stretched by a new experience can never go back to its old dimensions."*
> **OLIVER WENDELL HOLMES**

Why would you feel more alive and present when you brush your teeth with the opposite hand? It's not just because it's new. It's because it requires you to be fully present while you're doing it. If your mind wanders off, you will likely miss your teeth altogether and smear the toothpaste across the side of your face. You feel more alive because more of *you* — and therefore, less of the mechanical robot — is involved in the activity. Your mind hasn't drifted elsewhere, leaving the robot in charge.

But let's face it. You will likely go back to brushing your teeth with the hand you're used to. Totally fine. So how do you bring more aliveness to that and other routine, daily tasks? You do it by becoming the observer. Become the witness or the watcher of all that you think, feel, do and say. Do it as an experiment, as if you were an alien from another planet dropping in to watch you for an entire week. Watch how you do things and in what order. Watch how you put on a shirt. Be the observer. Watch your arm as it reaches for the shirt in the closet. Notice your hand as it takes the shirt off the hanger. Observe the movements of the body as you put the shirt on. It's fascinating! Don't make any judgments about what you are doing. There is no need to have a running commentary in your head. Simply watch.

Then try it with food. You're already eating two or three times a day, so meals are a wonderful opportunity to practice being the watcher or the observer. During your next meal, eat mindfully and with full awareness. Savor the food and the experience. Autopilot eating is not satisfying physically or emotionally. The robot eats more than the real you otherwise would.

> *"If you eat watchfully, food will become more tasty. Even ordinary food tastes good if you are watchful; and if you are not watchful, you can eat the most tasty food but there will be no taste in it because there is nobody to watch."*
> OSHO

Being the observer or the watcher automatically puts you in the present moment, which as we'll see in Chapter Twelve, is another key to lasting happiness and unplugging the robot for good.

GO ON AN ADVENTURE

> *"Jobs fill your pocket, but adventures fill your soul."*
> JAIME LYN BEATTY

> *"Because in the end, you won't remember the time you spent working in the office or mowing your lawn. Climb that goddamn mountain."*
> JACK KEROUAC

Adventure is the ultimate pattern interrupt. By definition, adventure takes you out of all-things-familiar and surrounds you with the new, the exciting and the unexpected. It is different from a guided tour or excursion where everything is taken care of in advance and you follow along. Nothing wrong in that, of course, but know that you're likely taking the robot along with you. An adventure is something more. It is about going beyond what is familiar and embracing the unknown.

You don't have to go on a safari or jump out of an airplane to feel more alive. Spending lots of money or traveling to distant lands is not required to have an adventure. You can experience adventure and newness anytime, anywhere. Leave the phone at home, get in your car and take a drive. Explore streets you've never been on. Drive until you get lost. Suddenly all your senses are alive. You are alert, absolutely alert. You are present in the here and now. What's the worst that could happen? You might actually have to interact with a person and ask for directions!

Virtually anything can become an exciting adventure, just by adding some novelty and a dash of the unknown to it. Even a simple thing like walking can offer a new dimension to your life. For me, walking has always served as a great source of adventure. I've walked 15 miles to get a haircut. Once I decided to walk to the office, all nine miles of it, while hilariously carrying my briefcase. I didn't map out the route in advance. I passed through neighborhoods I had never seen. I felt completely alive and present to the experience.

> *"A person who is alive, really alive, vitally alive, will always move into the unknown."*
> **OSHO**

> *"Who is the happier man, he who has braved the storm of life and lived or he who has stayed securely on shore and merely existed?"*
> **HUNTER S. THOMPSON**

How do you currently experience adventure? What adventures did you have as a kid? How might you incorporate that sense of exploration and discovery into your life now?

Feel free to revisit what you have written so far in your My Story of the Past and add to it any adventures or memories that may have surfaced. Our childhood is full of clues for understanding not only the programs that have shaped our beliefs and current habits but also the essence of what made us excited about being alive.

CHAPTER SEVEN

Unplug from the Mainstream

> "The fact than an opinion has been widely held is no
> evidence whatsoever that it is not utterly absurd."
> **BERTRAND RUSSELL**

Warning: this chapter might trigger you. People have strong opinions about the mainstream.

What is the mainstream and how is it different from conditioning? I use mainstream to refer to the norms and attitudes of society and the systems and underlying assumptions that support them. You can also think of it as the matrix or consensual reality. It includes the major industries that serve as the foundation to the way we live—government, the economic system, the mandatory school system, the medical industrial complex, the insurance system, the industrial agricultural system, the military industrial complex and the consolidated mainstream media. Since they are intricately related and support one another, they can collectively be referred to as The System or The Machine.

When you are plugged into the robot, you rarely question the validity or actual benefits of The System. Regardless of original intent, what we have now is a massive, money-driven machine that uses fear and manipulation to keep us plugged in and controlled. Don't think so?

Consider this: The System doesn't benefit from your eating exclusively pesticide-free, locally-grown food purchased at a farmers' market. Instead, with our tax dollars we subsidize industrial agriculture, genetically modified seeds and factory farming, which slaughters animals, depletes the soil and adds harmful hormones, chemicals and toxins to our food.

I warned you this chapter might trigger you.

The System doesn't want you to adopt a healthful lifestyle with regular time in nature, deep breathing, meditation, plenty of sleep, natural light, sunshine, fresh air and play—all of which are free. Instead, we are conditioned to believe that illness and disease can pounce upon us out of nowhere, that we are victims of our genes, that stress and pain are a normal part of life, and that deterioration of our body and mind is inevitable and only a matter of time. Adopting those beliefs supports both the pharmaceutical and insurance industries, as well as processed foodstuff manufacturers.

The System doesn't benefit from alternative sources of energy, many of which have been around for nearly 100 years. Instead, we subsidize inefficient automobiles and prop up crumbling transportation and energy infrastructures. To keep these systems in place—however antiquated and wasteful they may be—it is necessary to suppress inventions, censor information, marginalize alternatives and manipulate statistics. If something cannot be patented, and therefore controlled and monetized, it's best that you don't know about it.

Unplugging from the mainstream means examining some of the assumptions that lie beneath these systems. Regardless of what side of the political spectrum you are on, the current system called Government allows others to decide how your money is spent. By participating in the system called Medical Insurance, you allow strangers to decide which treatments and procedures are approved and how you manage your own body.

Our assumptions are, of course, a function of our conditioning as individuals. They are then reinforced collectively by society. Yet, *society* is not an independent thing. Society, government, organizations—these aren't individual sentient beings. They are just a bunch of people we group together under a label for convenience. In the case of society, it's a group we've consciously or unconsciously decided has more authority and knowledge than we do.

Who's the boss?

Do you ever wonder who *they* is when you hear someone begin a sentence with "they say?" Who is they? It can refer to society and it can also mean two or more people on the internet, so in essence, anyone. *They say* could be any random person regardless of credentials, intelligence or other qualifying factor. We might not know who actually said it, why or whether it is true, but using *they say* somehow lends it some authority.

The way we speak offers insights about our beliefs and assumptions as human beings. Terms of war, violence and competition infiltrate our language (notice my use of infiltrate just then). It's normalized and culturally acceptable to compete, take sides and have winners and losers.

- In business, we *battle* with the competition, devise new *strategies* to *defend our territory*, aim to *capture* a larger slice of the *target* market and hopefully, make a *killing* as a result.

- In our cities there is a *war* on drugs, a *war* on poverty and a *war* on crime. All of which have failed, by the way.

- In our bodies we *fight* disease. Our friend or relative *lost the battle* with this illness or that disease. Hospital workers have become *first-responders* on the *frontline*.

This is an unnecessary militarization of our common discourse that reinforces the notion that we have to be fearful and vigilant because enemies and Evil are everywhere. Language is a reflection of how we view ourselves. War metaphors reinforce the idea that there is an enemy to be conquered and that force and sacrifice are acceptable and required. And when we can't identify a clear enemy, we can always turn on ourselves as our own worst enemy in the form of self-sabotaging thoughts, beliefs and actions.

What we say and how we combine words matters. Like everything else, words have energy and send signals to our subconscious 24/7. Phrases such as "killing two birds with one stone," "kicking ass," "she's a fighter!" and "he crushed it" all imply that violence is good. And yet, when it comes to literally killing things, we use other terms and phrases to desensitize and distance ourselves from the act. Rather than eating the same animals you see in a zoo, we call it "livestock." We eat ham and bacon, not pigs. We order filet mignon and steak, not cow. Rather than trap and butcher an animal to consume it, the animal is "processed." It's our way of avoiding the discomfort of our actions.

Dig a little deeper and we discover other fundamental assumptions about how we view the world and our place in it. The mainstream story says "I am separate from you, we are separate from that country or culture over there, and humans are separate from and superior to nature." With this survival-of-the-fittest programming, we view the world through a filter of fear and scarcity. It doesn't have to be this way.

The current state of the world is a wake-up call for our own self-empowerment. We can move beyond the programming of fear and violence. We can learn to trust ourselves, our bodies, our feelings and our own capacity to see and know what is true. As I mentioned at the start of the book, unplugging the robot requires us to take responsibility—for our happiness, our body, our thoughts and our beliefs. Things are not always what they appear to be. We can live according to our own internal guidance rather than be steered by the opinions and fear programming of others. We are more than we've been taught to believe. We can become self-referencing and self-assured. The quickest way to do that is to unplug from the screen.

UNPLUG FROM THE SCREEN

> *"What we see on the screen is engineered to take something from us, extracting our data, attention or money."*
> DRS. DAVID AND AUSTIN PERLMUTTER, AUTHORS OF *BRAIN WASH*

The average American spends nearly half of her waking hours staring at a screen. Television, computers, smartphones, GPS, wearable electronic gadgets—the robot loves them. The more plugged in to digital devices you are, the harder it is to imagine what life would be like without instant internet searching and social media. While convenient and seemingly time-saving, our screens also do a marvelous job of keeping us distracted, addicted, reactive, passive and disconnected.

Distracted

Our phones have become weapons of mass distraction. It is increasingly rare to see someone waiting in line, dining in a restaurant or simply walking down the street without his or her phone at the ready. We think our phones and other digital devices increase our productivity, but most of our screen time is busyness we have created for ourselves. We allow constant surface distractions like texts, emails and social media to avoid unpleasant feelings we would rather not experience such as sadness, frustration, anger, boredom, jealousy, worry or dissatisfaction.

Playing online games, binge-watching shows or consuming the nightly news seem like harmless ways to entertain ourselves and relax after a long day. The reality is, we often use these activities to numb out and avoid our feelings. We unconsciously create outer distractions to keep our focus away from our inner anxiety, turmoil or unease.

> *"We are apt to get so caught up in the urgency of everything we have to do, and so caught up in our heads and in what we think is important, that it is easy to fall into a state of chronic tension, anxiety and perpetual distraction that continually drives our lives and easily becomes our default mode of operating."*
> JON KABAT-ZINN

Addicted

It is difficult to deny that we are addicted to our phones. Don't think you're addicted? Turn all of your phone notifications on, put your phone in a drawer and try not to open that drawer for 48 hours and see what happens. It is easy to understand why we are attached to the phone. Many of us use it as a watch, a camera, an alarm clock, a map, a day planner, even as a way to track how many steps we take in a day. We check the phone and react to it all day long.

We get a dopamine hit each time we reach for the phone to check in on social media or see what's happening. Many of us do this hundreds of times a day, reinforcing our addiction to likes, external validation, approval and the never-ending drama of the world. We have become conditioned Pavlovian reactors to every ring, ping and ding.

Reactive

The more plugged in you are, the more reactive you become. Just seeing your phone increases the level of stress hormones in your body. Reactions come from a place of fear or anxiety. They create a false sense of urgency and a fear of missing out on something. If you regularly watch news programming, for example, you'll be convinced it's a dangerous and scary world. A good portion of network news is negative, exaggerated and skewed. While we intuitively know the news channel doesn't contribute to our happiness or inner calm, we tell ourselves we watch it to stay informed.

Mainstream media is not in the information business. It is in the fear business. We're being polarized and manipulated to believe we are powerless. Controlled media gets us addicted to drama, which keeps us coming back for more. And then they sell us stuff. The goal of advertising, be it in magazines, online ads or commercials, is for us to feel fat, tired, ugly, sick, insecure, depressed or otherwise lacking. The commercials are cleverly designed to make us feel inadequate and to turn us into consumption robots. Ads reinforce a desire for instant gratification, the quick fix. We can purchase the solution right now. It's only a click away. On some level we know our problems will not magically be solved when we click "buy now," yet we click it anyway, over and over again. Of course, it always seems like a good idea at the time, which just proves how effectively we can be manipulated by marketing tactics.

Passive

Think of how much you do in a typical week that involves passively watching other people have an experience. Passive observer activities include anything you watch on a screen, such as television series, movies, sporting events, internet videos and social media clips. These screen-based activities suck you in as a passive observer of others' often imaginary lives.

As I mentioned in the introduction, it's not called a TV program for nothing. Whenever the television is on, you are being programmed, even if you are not actively watching it. Your subconscious mind absorbs and records all of it. That's why when you hear a song or advertising jingle from decades ago, you suddenly start singing all the lyrics without hesitation. It's all in there.

To feel more enthusiastic and fulfilled, it's *you* who needs the experience, not the robot that passively watches others have one. There is a difference between capturing something on your phone and experiencing it directly and digital-free. The two rarely happen simultaneously. Heightened aliveness and lasting happiness require your active participation. When you become a more active participant in your own life on all levels — physical, mental, emotional and spiritual — you will be amazed at how much time you really have to do, be and have all that you desire.

Disconnected

All that sedentary screen time takes a toll on our health. We become disconnected from our body and our intuition, which can distort our sense of reality. Our bodies are not designed to sit all day with our back hunched, chest caved in and head thrust forward. Our eyes are not meant to stare at close-range screens for hours at a time. Continuous sitting, poor posture and close proximity to screens drain your physical and mental energy.

We become disconnected and out of balance when technology starts to replace our human connections rather than augment them. It's increasingly common to confuse accessibility with connection.

Texting, instant messaging and social media are convenient, but they can't substitute being physically present with another person. It's the difference between an emoji hug versus an in-person 10-second one. The former offers a quick dopamine hit that ultimately leaves you dissatisfied and empty whereas the real body-to-body hug nurtures and energizes you on all levels.

Don't worry. I'm not suggesting we eliminate technology from our lives. The key is not letting your digital devices dominate your day. In my case, I used to check my phone the minute I woke up. I found myself increasingly stressed out and distracted by my inbox rather than focused on what I had intended for the day. No more. Now I wait at least an hour each morning before turning on the phone, so I can start each day with clarity, focus and calm. It's made a huge difference in both my productivity and my overall mood. If you currently check your phone first thing in the morning, try waiting an hour or until you get to the office instead. Go on a digital detox for a few days. It might feel weird and uncomfortable at first but it's worth it.

Challenge yourself to turn some of those screens off. Turn off the television. Disable the GPS. Resist the urge to look up everything online. Remember back in the good ole days when there was no GPS, no smartphones and no Google? Obviously, I am dating myself here, but the point is that while all those things are convenient, they take away the beauty of having to figure things out, of the adventure, the newness, the mystery, the *not knowing*. Driving to a new place without being told how to get there means you have to pay attention. You notice your surroundings. You are aware of things you would otherwise miss. You might have to strike up a conversation with another human. What an adventure!

OPT OUT

Just as you can opt out of 24/7 digital dependence, you can opt out of other robotic ways of being as well.

Back in the day, a friend used to describe me as a contrarian. Of course, I didn't agree with his characterization! I'm not against things for the sake of being against them. That's a waste of time and energy. But when it comes to things that make no sense whatsoever, I opt out. Body scanners in airports, for instance. I opt out. Doing so means I reduce my toxic load from electromagnetic radiation. Consumption events like Valentines' Day, Cyber Monday, Black Friday and St. Patrick's Day—I opt out of those too. A lot of what we call holidays—originally *holy days*—are now normalized days of robotic consumption and indulgence.

You can minimize your participation in The System. Alternatives already exist. There are independent health insurance collectives and effective treatments that don't require ongoing pharmaceuticals or invasive surgeries. There are plenty of schools that nurture a child's natural abilities. There are clean sources of food, clothing, building materials and energy that do not deplete the soil, damage your immune system or destroy the Earth. But you won't find them by consuming mainstream media or consulting mainstream search engines. Luckily, there are plenty of alternatives to those as well.

You have the power to opt out of The Machine and participate in more life-affirming options. You do this with your attention, your actions and your purchases. You can opt out of mainstream media and the fear, war-mentality and disempowerment that goes along with it. You can say goodbye to the nightly network news. Rest assured, if there is something you really need to know, your friends and family will tell you.

You can opt out of fear, competition and the illusion of scarcity. You can opt out of the consensus reality of endless doing, planning and rushing. Be a rebel. Forget about what everyone else is doing and what *they say*. Stop comparing yourself to others. You're not here on this planet to be like everyone else.

> *"Whenever you find yourself on the side of the majority, it is time to pause and reflect."*
> **MARK TWAIN**

Turn up the volume on your internal BS detector. Notice how words are used to influence your purchases and beliefs. The word *smart* is a perfect example, as in smart meter, smart speaker and smartphone. In these cases, smart means anything but. It's brilliant marketing, I'll admit. No one wants to question something that is smart. After all, it's smart, right? Not so fast. How can a beverage be smart if it's bottled in plastic? How can a home meter be smart if it involves more electromagnetic radiation than an analog one? How can a phone be smart if it contributes to our inability to think for ourselves, calculate basic math or organize our day? Now, don't misunderstand me. I, too, have a smartphone, but I am no smarter for it. I am acutely aware that anything that has to use smart as part of its name is suspect.

Consider where in your life you can opt out of things, systems, beliefs and even words that make no sense and are not in alignment with how you want to live.

CHAPTER EIGHT

Unplug from the Mind

> *"It isn't what you have or who you are or where you are or what you are doing that makes you happy or unhappy. It is what you think about it."*
>
> DALE CARNEGIE

As we've seen in the previous chapters, we are programmed from an early age to value our minds and our left-brain capacity to think, measure and analyze. We learn this in school and it is later reinforced in the workplace. It's no wonder, then, that we assume that our mind is who we are. The truth is, thoughts and beliefs are optional. Because we learn to internalize thoughts as ours, carry them with us and defend them, we believe we *are* our thoughts. Consider this: When you are sleeping or meditating deeply, for instance, you have no thoughts. Yet *you* still exist. If you have something or experience something, by definition you cannot be that something. You are the witness of it. Your thoughts are not you.

You can control what you do with your mind. When used consciously, the mind can be a wonderful tool. We can use it to plan, calculate and strategize. Unfortunately, most of us have given complete control over to the subconscious mind and it is using us. The mind jumps from thought to thought, keeping us scattered, busy and reactive with a steady stream of unimportant and unhelpful chatter. As a species we humans have evolved with a negativity bias. As such, we perceive our experiences from the old survival-based paradigm of fight or flight. Because the mind sees the world through a glass-half-empty filter, its chatter includes complaining, criticizing, comparing, rehashing the past and worrying about the future. The robotic mind distracts us with nonstop thoughts and emotional reactions, locking our focus on the external world that tells us what to do or buy to make us feel better.

The mind loves doing and drama. We derive pleasure in checking things off a to-do list, which trains our brain to create an endless to-do list simply for the pleasure of the checkmark! Because of this, we mistakenly associate frenetic activity and drama with a sense of aliveness. This is not real aliveness. As spiritual teacher Osho put it, *"keeping yourself busy is a kind of unconsciousness, is a kind of drug."*

Busyness is a trap. We become rushed, overcommitted and overworked, giving us a false sense of purpose, of *doing* something. We feel important. There is so much to do and only we can do it. Multitasking and other forms of addictive doing hold our mind in a state of chaos and can quickly spiral into overwhelm, anxiety and a scattered approach to life.

We can replace the false vitality we get from drama and busyness with the real aliveness that comes from within. When not actively using the mind as a tool for a specific task, we can set it aside. How do we do that? Conscious breathing, silence, meditation and superior thought focus are four ways to deactivate the robotic mind. Naturally, the mind will object to the suggestions below and point out dozens of reasons why they are impractical, naïve or stupid. Ignore that mind as you read on.

WAYS TO UNPLUG THE MIND

Conscious breathing

Conscious breathing and the monkey mind are utterly incompatible. When you activate one of them, you automatically turn the other one off. See for yourself. Focus on your breath, right now. Don't change the rhythm in any way. Just watch the breath. As you inhale, feel the air pass through your nostrils and allow your belly to expand. As you exhale, notice the air exiting your body as you pull in your belly toward the spine. Conscious breathing brings the scattered mind back to the here-and-now where everything is peaceful and harmonious.

Switch over to conscious breathing whenever you notice your mind on overdrive. Better yet, post reminders around the house and on your phone to unplug the mind with a few conscious breaths.

Silence

Do you regularly have the television or radio on for background noise? Do you listen to music while you drive, during a workout or while on the job? Maybe an alarm wakes you up every morning. Your phone likely pelts you all day long with notification sounds. External noise keeps us distracted, programmed and plugged into the robotic mind.

Luckily, we can instruct our minds to be still. Try sitting in silence for a moment and do nothing.

Go ahead, I'll wait.

How does it feel? Relaxing and peaceful? Or perhaps you feel antsy, bored, uneasy or irritable. Why does silence make so many of us uncomfortable? One reason is that we're trained to be doers, particularly in the West. Our addiction to doing means boredom and anxiety can set in when we find ourselves with nothing to do. Humans, by the way, are the only species that can experience boredom. Sitting in silence interrupts the compulsion toward busyness and external noise. When you practice silence, you open more space in your mind for new ideas and inspiration to come in.

Experiment with a few minutes of silence first thing in the morning and again at night. You don't even have to close your eyes. Sit comfortably, soften your gaze and relax your body. If a thought comes to you, simply observe it like a cloud passing by. Sit, relax, observe. That's it.

> *"There is nothing the mind can do that cannot be better done in the mind's immobility and thought-free stillness."*
> SRI AUROBINDO

Meditation

Once you develop a taste for sitting in silence, take it to the next level with meditation. Meditation is a powerful tool for relaxation, centering and unplugging the thought-robot. The key to meditation and other stillness practices is to allow thoughts or images to come and go without latching on to them and getting carried off down the mental rabbit hole. Don't try to stop thinking. The intention is to be with your inner self. If a thought comes up, just notice it. Be with whatever is occurring. You are the watcher, the observer, the essence behind your thoughts.

Superior thought focus

Superior thought focus is another way to unplug from the ordinary mind. Here, you consciously use your mind as a creative force. Whether you realize it or not, your thoughts influence people, things and the world around you. You are a nonstop broadcaster of your thoughts, so start directing your thoughts consciously. Whatever you think, you can create. Give your mind more empowering tasks and beliefs. Use the mind consciously to visualize, imagine and dream. Identify a code word to use to interrupt any negative thoughts and bring your focus back to what you want to create in your life.

In all four methods, awareness is the common denominator. With conscious breathing, you place your awareness on your breath. With silence, you become aware of the stillness and silence around you and beyond your thoughts. With meditation, you watch any thoughts that arise as you would clouds passing in the sky. With superior thought focus, you monitor your thoughts and reframe or redirect them to create your experience. In fact, awareness is its own strategy for unplugging the mind.

Awareness

Observing your mind as it thinks can add a whole new dimension to your life. With awareness, your everyday activities can become a moving meditation. As you go about your day, listen to your thoughts as if it were a podcast you've never heard before. You can determine if what you hear is relevant or helpful to you in that moment. Remind yourself that you are not that voice. How could you be? The very fact that you can hear it in your head, listen to it and observe it means that *it is not you*. You are the witness of it. As the observer, you can zoom out and watch the mind rather than be controlled by it.

Watch your reactions to people, circumstances and situations. Be on the lookout for what triggers you. If something happens and you get upset about it, that's the signal you've hit a trigger, otherwise known as a hidden wound. Reactions can include thoughts as well as emotions. It's the robot in you that emotionally reacts. In a reaction, *you* are not there.

Look for the sources of your conditioned behavior. Every time you become aware of the conditioned response in the form of a reactional thought or emotion, you neutralize part of your old programs. Use it as a reason to celebrate the fact that you noticed. With enough practice being aware and alert, you'll detect the reaction as it arises—or even before—rather than minutes or days later.

UPGRADE YOUR BELIEFS

Another way to unplug from the ordinary robotic mind is to question your beliefs. As we saw in *Chapter Five: Unplug from the Past*, our beliefs determine what is possible. What's the difference between a thought and a belief? A belief is a thought you think repeatedly. Therefore, to change your beliefs you must change your thoughts. Before you can do that, however, you've got to clarify a) what you believe and b) which of those beliefs interferes with your happiness.

Take stock of your physical environment, your body and the people you surround yourself with. Like it or not, your current circumstances are a mirror for what you believe. Consider the major sectors of your life, such as your health, family, friends, relationship, finances, career, spiritual life, etc. On an awesomeness scale of 1 to 10, what number would you assign to each? Beliefs that interfere with your happiness, aka limiting beliefs, occupy the space between you and a number 10 in each area.

We pick up many disempowering beliefs as children. Maybe you were repeatedly told "You can't make a living doing *that*" or "That's not how it works in the real world." Perhaps you had dreams of being a ballet dancer, an artist or an Olympian. Instead, you were told by well-intended others to be practical. Over time, you internalized those ideas as your own beliefs.

Identify what limits you

Before you can upgrade your beliefs, you need to realize what your beliefs are. Aside from viewing your current environment and circumstances as evidence of what you believe, monitoring your thoughts and your speech offers another window into your worldview. See if you resonate with any of these statements or remember hearing them as a child:

- It's good to keep busy.
- It takes 21 days to adopt a new habit.
- All good things must come to an end.
- Don't talk to strangers.
- Life is unfair.
- There is nothing you can do about it.
- There's not enough time in the day.
- Bigger is better.
- You are just like your *[brother, mother, stepfather, _____]*.
- Love never lasts.
- I am not good at *[meditation, money, relationships, _____]*.
- It's too late for me to *[change, find my dream job, find my soul mate, _____]*.

Common to many of these statements is victimhood, inadequacy and lack. There is victim programing in our collective experience. Even if you don't think of yourself as a victim, there still could be helplessness and hopelessness operating in the background of your life, hidden from view.

Now is a good time to take a look at what you've written in the My Story of the Past exercise from Chapter Five. See if you notice any limiting beliefs. They often take the form of if/only statements like "If only I could have gotten that job, then I would ____." They also include disempowering words such as can't, always, never, no, don't, won't, should, ought to and have to.

Some limiting beliefs are more subtle. Here's one: "My value as a person is a function of how much or what I do." Sit with that statement for a moment to see if it rings true for you. Perhaps you would not word it exactly like this, but chances are good you have taken on some version of this belief. We judge ourselves and others by how much we get done. If we do more, the programming goes, we just might feel good enough. To get good grades in school and be praised by others, we need to work harder. And if that isn't enough, you can do extra credit, meaning, work above and beyond, to feel good about yourself.

As adults, we ask kids, "What did you do today?" Not doing anything is seen as lazy, unproductive or a waste of time. Our everyday expressions reinforce this addiction to doing. We ask people, "How are you doing?" We don't ask anyone how she is be-ing. Questions like, "What do you want to be when you grow up?" are another way of asking "What are you going to *do* to make money?" We feel the need to justify our existence by explaining to others what we are doing. Notice if you have limiting beliefs about what or how much you do. Notice where you are tempted to use the word *should*.

Introduce doubt

Once you have a sense of what some of your limiting beliefs are, pick one that you would like to unplug from. Write it down. We begin to remove an old belief by introducing doubt. Ask yourself, is this belief really true? Zoom out from your day-to-day thinking and consider a wider perspective. Look for evidence where it is not true. Write down at least three situations or reasons why that belief or statement is not always 100% true.

Decide what you prefer

After inserting a wedge of doubt about your current belief, the next step is to choose a belief you prefer. Write down a list of positive, empowering beliefs you would like to adopt. As a starting point, take the limiting belief you identified and turn it around. For example, change the belief "I have to work hard and struggle to make money" into "I make money with ease doing the things I love." Be sure to state your new belief in the present tense and avoid negative words such as don't, not and never. Pick at least five empowering statements you would like to believe.

Change the programming

Installing new beliefs means rewiring your brain and creating new neural pathways to support the beliefs you prefer. You can do this with brain balancing exercises and by using all of your senses. Brain balancing exercises engage both sides of the brain to balance the left and right hemispheres. They help develop the pathways to support the beliefs you want. Here are two exercises to try:

- With your non-dominant hand, write down your new belief or draw a picture of it.
- Without moving your head, move your eyes slowly from side to side while you say the new belief.

Using all of your senses helps to install the new belief by engaging your body, mind and imagination.

- SIGHT: See the new belief in your mind's eye. Visualize it. Because the mind doesn't know the difference between what is imagined and what is real, we can reprogram it to look for evidence of how our new beliefs are true. See how the preferred belief is already true in the here and now.

- HEARING: Hear yourself say the affirmation aloud.

- TOUCH: Find a symbol or small object to represent the new belief and carry it around with you.

- TASTE: Write the belief on a slip of paper and tape it to the outside of a glass of water. Set the intention that the highest frequency of that new belief be programmed into the water. Then drink the water with awareness and appreciation.

- DREAM: Set the intention before bed to use sleep time to integrate the new belief and experience it as true.

Repetition

The more you imagine your preferred belief in vivid detail—as if it were happening now—the quicker you will train your mind to believe it.

- Review your list of new beliefs first thing in the morning to set the tone for the day.

- Regularly say your new belief aloud, while in the car, in the shower or before bed. But don't just mechanically read or say the words. Say it like you mean it. Smile and feel it in your body as true.

- Act as if it were already true now. How would the person who believes that speak and act?

- Practice new thoughts. How would the person who believes that think? Use superior thought focus we discussed in Chapter Eight.

- Write your new belief on a piece of paper and carry it around as a reminder.

Let's practice with another limiting belief. A common one is that it takes a specified length of time, such as 21 days or 90 days, to change a habit or belief. The truth is, change can happen in an instant. Change can be instantaneous if we want it badly enough. All it takes is to desire the new belief or state of being more than what we are currently doing and to consistently act according to that new belief. The robotic mind will, of course, dismiss this as ludicrous. Our mind loves lots of steps, milestones, goals and a lengthy progress. It gives it something to do.

I'll share a quick story. A few years ago, I attended a workshop in Europe. As everyone was getting acquainted around a large table, I noticed that a third of the people smoked. Trigger alert! Breathing and smelling cigarette smoke bothers me. Rather than be upset by this, I saw it as a choice point. An opportunity. I decided I was not going to let my long-held aversion and reaction to cigarette smoke interfere with my experience at the retreat. So, I consciously decided in that instant that cigarette smoke did not bother me. I changed my state of being in that very moment. It can really be that simple if you want it enough. It's the mind that's addicted to methods and lengthy exercises for change. If your life depended on it, you would do it.

"Hold on a minute," you might be thinking. "Didn't you say earlier that our subconscious programming is what's influencing our behavior 95% of the time? When our robot is in charge, yes. If you've read this far and done the suggested exercises along the way, it's unlikely your robot has the same level of control as when you started the book. That's the beauty of awareness. Once you know the truth of something, it's difficult to un-know it.

But back to my story and the belief that it takes a certain amount of time to change. As we saw in my cigarette smoke example, change can be instantaneous if the desire for the new belief is strong enough. However, changing our habits, thoughts and reactions for good requires more than a decision. It's not solely a matter of applying willpower. For change to be lasting or permanent, we also need repetition and consistent practice. After my smoke-filled workshop overseas, I didn't practice my new-found indifference to cigarette smoke back home. In fact, I forgot all about it.

The neural pathways in our brain are set by repetition. When we change our thoughts and practice the new ones repeatedly, we create pathways for the new beliefs to take hold. Feeling the beliefs as true in our body allows the new neural networks to form even faster.

Use this four-part process—introduce doubt, decide what you prefer, change the programming and repetition—to upgrade other limiting beliefs you have identified.

PART THREE

CONNECT TO THE REAL YOU

Connect to the Real You

"It's the moments that I stopped just to be, rather than do, that have given me true happiness."
SIR RICHARD BRANSON

"Be who you are and say what you feel, because those who mind don't matter, and those who matter don't mind."
BERNARD BARUCH

As we saw in the last chapter, our mind likes to make things complicated. The mind is goal-oriented and views change of any kind as a long and arduous process. According to the mind, if something is easy or free, it must be too good to be true. It believes value comes from struggle and effort.

Luckily for us, the robotic mind is wrong. Lasting happiness doesn't cost anything and you already have it. Happiness comes from embodying and expressing who you are at the core. The formula is quite simple:

- Step One: Unplug the robot, which is all the Not You (i.e., the conditioning, the stories and the unhelpful beliefs we've explored thus far).

- Step Two: Connect to the real you underneath that's been waiting to emerge all along.

What does the real you look like? The real you is love, joy and beauty. Playful and free. The real you thrives on connection, intimacy, belonging, cooperation and collaboration. The real you values service, humility and generosity. The true self, the real you, doesn't judge, compete or take sides. The real you is curious, enthusiastic, intuitive, energetic, radiant, vast and unlimited. The real you is the one who dances, sings, paints and creates.

How do I know this?

Because those things are in everyone. It is part of our humanness. Our human nature goes beyond the five senses of sight, hearing, taste, touch and smell. Each of us is born with intuitive abilities and multidimensional awareness. We forget this by the time we enter the schooling system and develop left-brain dominance, but they are still there. We are a unique expression of the unified field that connects everything with everything.

> *"What is normal is enthusiasm. What is normal is laughing a lot. Many, many times a day. Feeling strong and secure.... What is normal is a zest for life beyond anything that most of you, over eight years old, have remembered or felt in a long, long time. That's what's normal."*
> **ABRAHAM-HICKS**

We humans have forgotten who we are and why we are here. As we saw from the My Story of the Past exercise, the labels, occupations, circumstances, roles and habits we adopt are not who we are. They are only what we have experienced thus far. The midlife crisis, the accident and the illness—these are not events that define us. They are wake-up calls from our innermost core, telling us that we are out of harmony with ourselves, our body, with nature or with life itself.

The real you is the part who asks, "Is this the life I really want to live? Is this it?"

In *Part Two: Pull the Plug*, we explored how childhood conditioning, inherited programs and societal and cultural norms have influenced our thoughts and beliefs about what is possible. Here in *Part Three: Connect to the Real You*, we change all that. We invite the real you to come forward. We do this by connecting with intuition, our heart and with nature herself.

CHAPTER NINE

Connect with Your Intuition

> *"Intellect is the functioning of the head, instinct is the functioning of your body and intuition is the functioning of your heart."*
> OSHO

Despite what you may have learned growing up, it's not your mind or brain that makes the best decisions. It is your intuition.

> *"Your mind wants you to believe that acknowledging your intuition is impractical, a waste of time, and possibly dangerous, and it will do everything to keep you distracted."*
> SONIA CHOQUETTE

Intuition is the ability to understand something immediately, without the need for conscious reasoning. It is your inner guidance system, the powerhouse of inner knowing. Intuition is unique to you. It's that gut feeling or knowing that something is right or something seems off. It's the small voice that tells you to get that mole checked out even when everyone around you tells you it's nothing. It's the feeling you get when you just know someone is not telling the truth. Intuition serves as your personal BS detector.

All of us have intuition. As babies and young children, we were fully connected with our intuition. Unfortunately, over time we slowly override it with external influences such as family, friends, society, church and school. We learn to ignore it, diminish it or bury it with thoughts and logic. By the time we are adults, we have piled so much "life garbage" on top of our internal guidance system and natural intuitive abilities that we no longer have easy access to them.

It doesn't have to be this way. You can tap into this incredible guidance system to help you navigate every moment of the day.

THE LANGUAGE OF INTUITION

Understanding intuition means first determining how your intuition communicates with you. Intuition is all about subtlety, which is why so many of us miss it. Our intuition patiently waits for us to slow down, pay attention and notice how it operates. It could be through feeling, emotion or an idea that pops into our head. Intuition speaks through sight, sound, knowing and feeling.

If sight is the dominant modus operandi for your intuition, you might see pictures or scenes in your mind's eye. If your intuition primarily communicates via sound, you could hear words or phrases in your head. With knowing and feeling, you know something to be true without thinking about it or analyzing it. You feel the intuitive insight in your body. You might get a physical sensation in your gut when something is true and aligned or when something feels wrong and off. When well-developed, our intuition speaks to us using all of these methods, although there's often a dominant one.

How do you know which method is dominant for you? Try this—What happens when I ask you this question:

What are you most passionate about?

How did the answer come to you, before your mind kicked in and started thinking about it? Did you *hear* the answer in your head, *see* it in your mind's eye, *feel* it in your body or just *know* it? The way your answer came to you is a clue to how your intuition currently communicates with you.

Accessing your inner GPS is a bit like remembering a foreign language you were exposed to as a child but have since forgotten. It doesn't matter if you haven't used the language in 20 years and believe the skill is long gone. It is still in there. So is your intuition. With practice, you can develop each of the four channels for receiving intuitive insight.

The more cerebral you are, the harder it can be to access your internal guidance at first. That was my challenge when I started. Being too much in my head was an obstacle to accessing my intuition and trusting what I received. I had to constantly remind myself to stop, slow down, tune in and listen. It took practice to become aware of where I felt intuition in my body and how that differed from how the mind speaks.

In my work with clients, a common question I get is, "How do I know if a thought is coming from my intuition or my mind?" Intuition sounds and feels different than when your mind tells you something. Intuition feels good. It is your body and soul speaking to you. Anything that feels negative, heavy, constricting or doubtful is likely your mind. The mind often speaks in terms of "should," "ought to," "have to" or in judgments and complaints. The ordinary mind is loud and can be hard to turn down. Intuition is quieter and more subtle. When coming from the mind, the body tends to tighten and contract. When it's coming from intuition, the body feels open and expansive.

PREPARE TO CONNECT

Now that you know the language of intuition and how it differs from the robotic mind, it's time to practice connecting with it. Sit in a chair with your feet on the floor. Close your eyes. Select an issue where you would like guidance. Set an intention to receive intuitive insights about the issue of concern. It helps to expect to receive an answer. Then let it go. Relax into the silence, yet remain alert. Listen and observe. Stillness allows for the space and quiet to access your deeper knowing. You are not trying to think of a solution. You are also not trying to *not* think. Become aware of all of your senses and tune in to your body. Does your body feel light or heavy? Expansive or contracting? Notice whatever comes up. It could be that nothing comes up. That's fine too. If thoughts pop in, notice them and let them float by. After a few minutes, write down your impressions.

How did it go? Did you observe your thoughts as an impartial observer or did you latch on to a thought and get carried away in the current? Learning to access and trust your intuition takes practice, so don't be concerned if you didn't receive an immediate answer regarding your issue. Pay attention over the next day or two and be on the lookout for signs and messages from your intuition.

Another form of practice is to ask for inner guidance before going to sleep. Dreams can be a fascinating source of intuitive guidance. They can include messages from your subconscious or from your higher self. One trick for remembering your dreams is to set an intention to do so. As you lie in bed, ready to fall asleep, silently state something like this: "I intend to vividly remember only those dreams that offer guidance for my best and highest good." Keep a pad of paper near the bed to record your dreams first thing in the morning, even before your feet touch the floor.

Another technique to improve dream recall is take a large glass of water and drink half of it before going to bed. When you wake up in the middle of the night to go to the bathroom, quickly jot down whatever you remember from your dreams. Then drink the rest of the glass and go back to sleep. For best results, keep pen and paper handy in the bathroom as well.

TAKE ACTION

Building a relationship with your intuition takes more than tuning in here and there. It takes regular practice and a willingness to trust the guidance you receive. Take action on your intuitive hits. Start with small things. You'll soon come to know your intuition as the personal round-the-clock advisor it was meant to be.

CHAPTER TEN

Connect with Nature

"And into the forest I go, to lose my mind and find my soul."
JOHN MUIR

Happiness means being fully alive and connected. Both require nature.

We *are* nature. We are made up of the same elements as the Earth. It makes sense, then, that the more time we spend cut off and isolated from nature inside our homes, offices and cars, the more disconnected and "off" we feel. Here in the West, we live an astonishing 90% of our day inside man-made structures. Because of this physical separation from the outdoors, we become disassociated from the natural world, leading us to think we can live perfectly fine without nature. We can't.

"We have become trees that are uprooted—and nobody else is responsible except us, with our own stupid idea of conquering nature. We are part of nature—how can the part conquer the whole?"
OSHO

We need the sun, not just shining *over there*. Shining on us. It's well documented that lack of sunshine and fewer daytime hours contribute to anxiety and depression. Back in my corporate days in the Midwest, I left for the office in the winter mornings in darkness and it was dark again before the commute home. Not only did my day begin and end in darkness, but I also spent the time in between in a gray-paneled cubicle with no windows, plants or decoration of any kind. Pretty soon my mood and outlook mirrored that grayness and darkness.

Our bodies need sun and natural light without sunglasses, chemicals or other barriers. Yet we've been taught to fear the sun and cover ourselves with multiple forms of protection. According to Dr. Jacob Liberman, author of *Light: Medicine of the Future*, a surprising two-thirds of the energy produced by the body comes from natural light, whereas only one-third comes from food. It's only recently in the human experience that we've become indoor creatures. Our true nature is outdoors.

> *"Over time, too many of us have lost a sense of who we are in relation to both the physical world and to other living beings, human and otherwise, who share the same space."*
> RICHARD LOUV, AUTHOR OF *OUR WILD CALLING*

We've been taught to see the natural world as objects to be taken and used as we see fit. We actually refer to them as natural resources. (Never mind that we consider people as *human resources*.) We have become disassociated from nature, in part because what we are doing to the Earth is so horrific that it is too much to reconcile. We cut down the forests. We pollute the ocean. And while you and I aren't personally cutting down the trees or slaughtering animals, our daily choices and consumption behaviors drive those activities. Part of unplugging the robot is acknowledging this and changing our relationship with nature from one of extraction and exploitation to one of sacred reciprocity, where we regularly give back to Earth as a normal part of everyday life.

Connecting with nature also means connecting with our body—the amazing vehicle we borrow while here on this planet. That body is designed for movement: to walk, run, reach and play. Our bodies are not meant for prolonged sitting inside a house, apartment or office building. It is not natural to sit in a man-made box, staring for hours at a time at our handheld phone box, the computer box or other four-cornered screen. Have you ever noticed that there are no squares or box-shaped things in nature? The square doesn't exist in nature precisely because *it is not natural.* Boxes and squares are human inventions. Notice how there are no squares or corners on the human body either.

Our body is designed to move and play. I'm not referring to exercise. Exercise is a man-made activity we do for an isolated block of time, perhaps a few hours a week, so our bodies don't fall apart. Exercise helps us manage the other 100+ hours spent stationary in a chair.

Movement is different than exercise. Movement is part of our nature. It's how we live and play throughout the day: squatting, reaching for things, dancing, playing. When was the last time you went outside to play? We need play. Outdoors. Genuine play includes activities and games that don't have rules decided in advance by others. Play isn't about competition or winning. It's about the sheer joy that comes from engaging in an activity *for its own sake.* It involves exploration, discovery, wonder, silliness.

The more time we spend outdoors in nature, the quicker we regain the ability to feel awe and see the magic and mysterious perfection of life. We can recapture the curiosity and wonder we knew as a child. All of nature is alive and ready to teach us—the trees, the animals, the insects, even the rocks.

> *"Be amazed and astonished by the flow of the river, the blueness of the sky, the smile of a child, the stillness of a peaceful morning. Yet we must not simply wait for something to generate a sense of awe in us. We can rise above being stimulus-response animals and cultivate our own emotions, steering our free will into creating a sense of awe within our being. In this moment, I can simply decide to feel awe at the wonders of this universe."*
> **BRENDON BURCHARD**

We humans are not the pinnacle of creation. We are one species among millions sharing this planet. We are interconnected with the plants, the animals, the elements and all of life. Nature is our greatest teacher. We are the last thing created, which means we have the most to learn from our surroundings. Our assignment here is to support and enhance all life. We are stewards of the Earth. We are meant to be its caretakers.

Connecting with nature—or with a single tree in your yard—makes it easier to access the inner peace and calm that is always within us. The mind quiets down. We see things from a wider lens. We sense and feel more. We feel more alive in nature because that is where the real aliveness is. Plug into the natural world. Connect with the land. Explore and discover how nature speaks. Stargaze, forest bathe, read a book under a tree. Picnic with real food, plant a small garden or help a friend or neighbor tend to theirs. Place real plants in your home and talk to them. Connect with animals and trees. Surround yourself with nature. Your nature *is* nature.

CHAPTER ELEVEN

Connect to the Heart

"Our days are happier when we give people a bit of our heart rather than a piece of our mind."

UNKNOWN

As we saw in *Chapter Eight: Unplug from the Mind*, we are taught to live from our heads. We repeatedly think about the past and judge ourselves and everyone around us through the lens of our past experiences. We also obsess about possible future scenarios, most of which never actually happen. Often without realizing it, we allow our minds to run our lives.

Lasting happiness doesn't come from the mind. Fulfillment and joy come from the heart. When you connect with your heart and live more of your day from that space, you can access the kindness, compassion and love that lie at the core of your being.

KINDNESS

"If you want happiness for an hour, take a nap. If you want happiness for a day, go fishing. If you want happiness for a year, inherit a fortune. If you want happiness for a lifetime, help someone else."

CHINESE PROVERB

We are hardwired for kindness, yet our subconscious programs and cultural conditioning often override this natural tendency. Kindness is important not because *it's the right thing to do* or because *it makes you a good person*. No. That type of thinking is part of our conditioning. Kindness matters because it contributes to your own happiness and self-transformation. And as a bonus, it positively impacts others. When you acknowledge someone else's kindness, for instance, or say thank you whenever possible, you add to the beauty of all that is. You feel great. You help others. Anyone who happens to witness your kind act is also uplifted. Seeing an act of kindness reminds us that we are all connected. It renews our faith in the goodness of human nature.

How can we connect to the heart and bring our natural kindness to the surface? One way is to become still and connect with your body. Direct your attention and awareness inward. Visualize breathing from the heart space. Consider it an act of kindness toward your mind and body as you follow the breath into your heart and follow the breath out from your heart.

Another way to bring our inner kindness out is to engage in deliberate acts of kindness. Deliberate acts of kindness are different from random ones. The random variety are exactly that—random. We don't know when we might feel inspired to smile at someone for no reason, pay it forward or give a genuine compliment. Deliberate acts of kindness require intent, a bit of front-end planning and actively looking for opportunities to be of service.

Let's do that now. Take out a sheet of paper and make a list of random acts of kindness you have done in the past. Now get creative. What is something that could brighten someone's day that would push you beyond your current comfort zone? Here are some ideas to get you started:

- While driving, happily allow anyone to merge into your lane.
- Smile at your coworkers, look them in the eye and say good morning.

- Acknowledge people you pass on the street with a nod, a smile or a hello.

- Pick up litter in the park.

- Call a friend you would normally text.

- Offer a sandwich to someone in need.

- Let someone go ahead of you in line at the grocery store, especially if they have more items than you do.

- Mail a hand-written note or an inspirational book to a friend.

- Listen to someone with your full attention, which means no multitasking or thinking of what you will say next.

- Leave something nice on your neighbor's doorstep.

- Compliment a stranger's smile, clothes, garden or dog.

- Think of creative ways to strike up a conversation with new people, such as "accidently" dropping something of yours near them.

"The happiness of life is made up of the little charities of a kiss or smile, a kind look, a heartfelt compliment."
SAMUEL TAYLOR COLERIDGE

We usually think of random acts of kindness in terms of the other person. To really unplug the robot and engage the heart, however, we must regularly engage in the radical act of *self*-kindness. That's right. A beautiful, peaceful and happy world starts by cultivating our own inner peace, self-kindness and self-love.

Grab that sheet of paper and make a second list. This one is all about you. Write down ways you could show genuine kindness to yourself, such as:

- Respect your body by eating only the highest quality, organic food this week.

- Nurture yourself with a bubble bath or two extra hours of sleep.

- Do something you normally wouldn't do, like buy yourself flowers, have breakfast in bed or turn off your phone for 48 hours.

- Engage in an activity that makes you feel more alive, such as dancing, hiking, yoga, sports, stargazing or coloring.

- Nourish your mind with positive thoughts, creative projects or a good chunk of silence.

- Initiate uplifting conservations with loved ones.

- Cook something with love and kindness for yourself, then eat it slowly with gratitude.

Now pick something from both lists that you will do this week. Write them on a piece of paper and carry it with you everywhere as a reminder. When you pay attention and actively look for opportunities to share kindness, you'll soon notice your surroundings in a new way.

> *"The best portion of a good man's life is his little, nameless, unremembered acts of kindness and of love."*
> **WILLIAM WORDSWORTH**

Practice gratitude and kindness especially when you don't feel like it. Daily practice rewires your brain. You become more positive and optimistic. You begin to see the glass as half-full instead of half-empty. Every thought and action coming from a place of kindness, love and compassion plays an important role in shifting the collective programming of fear, separation and scarcity to one of genuine kindness and generosity. You boost your level of happiness and contribute to the world.

COMPASSION

> *"Since we desire the true happiness that is brought about by a calm mind, and such peace of mind arises only from having a compassionate attitude, we need to make a concerted effort to develop compassion."*
> **DALAI LAMA**

Compassion is a powerful way to connect to the heart and the real you. What exactly is compassion? Compassion comes from acknowledging that if you were in the other person's shoes, you would do the same thing they did. "Now wait a minute," you might be thinking, "there's no way I would ever do *that* as president of the country or owner of that corporation. I would never kill that person, destroy that forest or raise my kids that way." Newsflash: Yes, you would. If you were in that person's shoes, thinking their thoughts, living their life, enveloped in their past, you would likely do the same thing.

Other people's lives are more complicated than they appear from the outside. Think about that for a moment. Why do we believe our own lives are so much more complicated? Because we can't see or know what's going on internally in others. We only see what's on the outside. Since we can't think other people's thoughts or feel their emotions, we make the common mistake of comparing our internal stuff with everyone else's external stuff.

In my own life, I vividly remember saying to myself, "Why would she do that?" or "I would never do that," only to have my own circumstances change years later where I got a glimpse of what that person might have been going through. It was a humbling experience. I realized you can never know the totality of someone's story or step inside their head to hear what their inner dialog has been all their life. That means you can't blame anyone for anything. Just like you, everyone else downloaded early programming they didn't choose, so there's no point in blaming, condemning or judging people. What other people say and do makes perfect sense to them based on their framework, upbringing, filters, conditioning, beliefs and level of awareness. If you were in their shoes, as that person, it would make sense to you as well.

Despite what we may think about other people and the views they hold, at bottom we are much more alike than different. The next time you are tempted to judge someone, imagine what it must be like to be them, what must have happened in their lives, in their families, to think or act as they do.

The key to compassion is realizing you can't put yourself in someone else's shoes. You'll never know the full story. When you truly grasp this, deep down in your bones, it can change how you see everything, including yourself, your family and the world around you. You begin to embody genuine compassion, which then unlocks the power of the heart.

Compassion takes practice. It means being kind to yourself first and foremost. Develop an unconditional friendship with yourself. Whatever happened in the past no longer matters. Had you known differently or had a different mix of life experiences, you would have chosen or done differently. The whole notion of regrets is a waste of your life force and a waste of your Now.

Pause for a minute or two to connect again with your body. Visualize breathing in and out from your heart. Engage the heart in this way as often as possible to allow your brain to become synchronized with it.

LOVE

> *"Happiness cannot be traveled to, owned, earned, won or consumed. Happiness is the spiritual experience of living every minute with love, grace and gratitude."*
> **DENIS WAITLEY**

As they reach the end of their lives, the elderly have the same 2-3 regrets. They did not wish they had more stuff or got more things done. What they regret most was not spending more time with their family and friends. Not taking more risks. Not loving more.

Love is critical for health and happiness. Yet, as with happiness and compassion, love is an inside job. It starts from within. So let me ask you, do you love yourself? If the question makes you uncomfortable, you are not alone. It's not a common topic of conversation. Perhaps you never genuinely contemplated whether you truly love yourself— your quirks, your perceived imperfections, all your bits and pieces. Ponder it now. Do you love it all unconditionally?

Why is it so hard to love ourselves? As you might expect, we can look to our cultural conditioning for clues. Maybe love was never discussed in your family. We certainly did not learn to love ourselves in school. Quite the opposite. We're trained to compare and compete with others and criticize ourselves. We proved our worth with grades and medals. We wanted approval from our parents, teachers and friends. And now as adults, we use phrases like "earn a living," which implies that you have to work hard to justify your very existence. It's no wonder we don't love ourselves.

> *"When you truly love and accept yourself as you are, you won't care so much about the approval of others."*
> **DAN MILLMAN**

Loving yourself is a radical act. It means respecting and honoring your body, your commitments, your values. Here's the thing about self-love. A lot of us don't understand it. Our mind can't quite wrap itself around the concept. For many of us, self-love seems weird, foreign — something done only in New Age groups, like prolonged eye-gazing. The truth is, love is essential for living fully and robot-free.

> *"You can love others only if you are able to love yourself. But society condemns self-love. It says it is selfishness, it says it is narcissistic."*
> **OSHO**

Self-love starts with acceptance. Accepting what already is. Accept yourself for who and how you are, right now. If something is happening, assume it's supposed to be happening. That doesn't mean you can't change it. It doesn't even mean you have to like it. Acceptance means not resisting this moment. It already *is*, so resistance is futile. When you accept the moment that's happening, you can approach it from an empowered place rather than a victim-based one.

Self-love requires you to believe you are worthy of love. This is a big one. Do you believe that, just by virtue of existing, you are worthy? It's nearly impossible to grow up in this day and age and not feel insufficient, incomplete or unworthy in some way. Modern society does not encourage us to love and approve of ourselves. According to some religious teachings, we are all born sinners. According to government institutions and the medical establishment, we are incapable of knowing what's best for ourselves or making informed decisions, so we need to be told what to do. According to what we see in films, magazines and online, we are overweight, unattractive and altogether lacking, and our not-enoughness can be solved with a purchase. It's absurd. Lasting happiness does not come from anything external. It comes from an internal sense of belonging here, knowing and feeling that we are good enough.

There is nothing to prove. You are part of the whole and logically speaking, if you aren't worthy, then nothing is. Creation doesn't make mistakes. The fact that you are here, in this body, on this planet, at this moment in time, makes you worthy. You automatically qualify. You may have to return to this paragraph repeatedly for that to sink in. Consider writing it on a piece of paper. Post it on your bathroom mirror or carry it with you. Use the exercises outlined in Chapter Eight to instill the belief that you are worthy and deserve love. That you *are* love.

Practice kindness and compassion as acts of self-love. Try this exercise: Think of three things you appreciate about yourself. Does even the thought of acknowledging or appreciating yourself sound vain or boastful? It isn't. Write down three things you genuinely like about yourself. Allow yourself to feel good about those things for at least 60 seconds. Then review your list before bed. Set the intention that while you are asleep you will fully integrate those three qualities and experience internal validation from them. When you wake up the next morning, review the list again and add three more things to it. Don't ask anyone for suggestions. The three things have to come from you. Repeat this process for 10 days, so by the end of it you have a list of 30 things. It's a powerful method to develop kindness toward yourself and to remember your innate value and unique expression.

Another technique to practice self-love is through affirmations. Back in the 1990s there was a popular Saturday Night Live skit called "Daily Affirmations with Stuart Smalley." Stuart would sit in front of a mirror and say things like "I'm good enough, I'm smart enough, and gosh darn it, people like me." People thought it was hilarious. It was widely imitated. Unfortunately, it reinforced the idea that saying affirmations was something only weirdos did. While the skit's popularity was indicative of the culture at the time, we still feel foolish saying nice things to ourselves.

Whether we realize it or not, each of us is constantly affirming something. Our thoughts offer a nonstop commentary of how we view ourselves and the world. Yet when used consciously, affirmations can be a powerful tool for transforming disempowering beliefs into loving ones. With repetition, affirmations can create new neural pathways in the brain to turn the affirmation into a new belief.

Pick a positive statement about yourself or your circumstances. Write down your affirmation in the present tense, keep it short and avoid negative words such as don't, not and never. "I deserve to be happy" is a good one to start with. Now, incorporate this affirmation into your life in as many ways as possible. Say it to yourself first thing in the morning and last thing at night. Write the phrase down 100 times, preferably with your non-dominant hand to engage both hemispheres of the brain. Now don't misunderstand me. It's not enough to mechanically repeat the phrase or write it down like a robot. You've got to feel it as true to get results. Imagine how it would feel to be the person who wholeheartedly believes he deserves to be happy.

FEEL

Speaking of feelings, allowing yourself to feel your emotions—all of them—contributes to self-love. With love at one end of the emotional spectrum and fear at the other, it's common to focus on what we perceive to be "good" or "positive" emotions and push away the "bad" ones we don't want. Emotions don't work that way. Emotions are simply energy in motion. Like the waves in the sea, an emotion comes in and then it goes out. They are designed to move through us. Young kids know this. They can cry hysterically for three minutes and then it is over and done with. They quickly resume laughing and playing as if nothing happened.

Because emotions like anger and grief are painful, we often block their natural path through the body so we don't have to feel them. We ignore the emotion, suppress it or cover it up with addictions or distractions such as food, digital devices, work and video games. Our consumer society encourages us to do this. Without an outlet, those emotions of frustration or anger become buried in the body.

We are meant to feel and process our emotions, not suppress them or unleash them on others. The ideal scenario is this: We sense an emotion, acknowledge it, allow ourselves to feel it through to completion and then release it. It doesn't matter if the emotion seems silly or insignificant. Acknowledge its presence anyway. For example, you could say to yourself, "That leaf blower is annoying!" or "I am mad!" Then accept it. Be okay with the fact that the emotion is there. Become curious about it. This emotion could be trying to tell you something. Tune in and ask your body. What might be the unmet need behind it? Sit with it so you can feel the emotion all the way through.

You release an emotion by feeling it and expressing it. We can express our emotions in a healthy way. Have a good cry, go for a run, get a punching bag or scream into a pillow. Get your body moving. Dance, jump, shake it out. Visualize the energy moving out through the bottom of your feet and down into the core of the Earth where it is instantly neutralized. Then reconnect with your heart space—where your essence of kindness, compassion and love reside.

CHAPTER TWELVE

Connect to the Present

"The miracle is not to walk on water. The miracle is to walk on the green earth, dwelling deeply in the present moment and feeling truly alive."
THICH NHAT HANH

You may have heard how being in the present or being in the moment contribute to greater happiness. But what does that really mean? It may sound obvious, but you miss the present moment when you use it to think about the past, the future or "what's next." Let's examine each of these scenarios.

PAST

"As you walk and eat and travel, be where you are. Otherwise you will miss most of your life."
BUDDHA

Abiding in the present means not using the Now to think about, ponder or dwell on the past. Since you can't do anything about what has already happened, habitually placing your attention on it serves no purpose. Mulling over the past guarantees that you miss the current moment you are in. What's more, engaging repeatedly with *what was* drags those past events and circumstances into the future, which is why history tends to repeat itself.

FUTURE

> *"Tomorrow does not happen—it has never happened. It is simply a stupid strategy of postponement. What happens is always today."*
> OSHO

Being in the present means not worrying about the future or contemplating "what if" scenarios of what someone might do, how the government might change or where the stock market is headed. Planning too much, overthinking, analyzing and setting detailed goals for the future overrides the Now. It creates expectations of how things should go, thereby limiting your ability to see new, exciting and often better opportunities that surround you in this moment.

We're conditioned to be fearful about what *might* happen. Our collective story teaches us that happiness is always around the corner or off on the horizon, after we have done this or purchased that. The reality is, happiness is already here now, in the moment we are in.

NEXT

This is the most insidious distraction from the present. When we constantly think about what we're going to do next, once again we miss the present moment. Present moment awareness isn't about thinking at all. Thinking, planning and strategizing are techniques the mind employs to feel in control. I'll admit, I was once an obsessive planner. Then I noticed I was often living in the next 10 minutes or two hours ahead. I still catch myself doing this—living in my head rather than in the moment with the experience directly in front of me. I vividly remember wondering recently about what I was going to eat later on for dinner, as I was in the middle of having lunch! There I was, completely missing the experience that was occurring—my eating a tasty meal I prepared— because *I was not there*. The robot was the one eating. This is what I'm referring to when I said we humans live mostly in and from our heads. My experience was essentially mentally pondering my next, not-yet-here experience. What a waste.

When we mentally rehash the past or rehearse the future, what's certain is this: we miss this present moment. When we miss the present moment, the robot has taken over. Connecting to the present means staying alert and awake in this moment, the one happening now. How do we do this? Three ways: 1) Pay attention to your body, 2) Go with the current and 3) Remember death. Let's examine each of these three methods.

HOW TO CONNECT TO THE NOW

Pay attention to your body

The body is constantly trying to get your attention. Tune into it now. Take a few deep breaths from your heart space. Connect with your internal guidance system. Recall the four methods we covered earlier about how intuition speaks to you: via sight and your mind's eye, as internal sound, as a physical sensation or as a knowing.

Use your body to ground and anchor you in the here and now. Close your eyes and do a sensory internal scan through the body. Start at the top of your head. Notice any sensation. Then move to your forehead, your eyes, your lips. Now to your neck, your shoulders. Continue down through the body. Include your bones and your organs. Notice what is going on in your body.

Unfortunately, most of us only notice our body when something hurts. You stub your toe, for instance, and suddenly all of your focus is directed to the foot. How often do you notice the foot when it doesn't hurt? Make it a regular practice to check in with your body at least once a day. Become familiar with it. The body is a beautiful mystery, engaging in thousands of functions day after day, yet many of us don't have a basic knowledge of our own anatomy. Could you point to your gallbladder or your pancreas? Full disclosure—until recently, I couldn't either.

Engage your body as you would a partner. Get to know it's preferences and quirks. Notice when you are breathing from your chest rather than from your belly. Pay attention to the body's cues.

Go with the current

Think back to when you were really in the flow, where time seemed to stop, where you were completely engrossed in something. Nothing else mattered. You were in the Now. When you go with the current, you go with the natural flow of life. That doesn't mean dumping all structure and responsibility and going along with just anything. Going with the current means not resisting what's already happening.

Maybe you had your day planned out in intricate detail and something or someone popped up and seemingly ruined it all. So what if there's a sudden change of plans? The robot in us wants to react and become upset. Emotional reactions are ways we unconsciously drag the past along with us to cloud the present. Stay alert. It's an unplug opportunity! Return to the moment.

> *"You can only be here now when you instantly accept emotionally whatever happens in your life."*
> **KEN KEYES, AUTHOR OF** *HANDBOOK TO HIGHER CONSCIOUSNESS*

There is no point to resisting life's events. We cannot do anything about them. They are already happening, so why not go with them? Go with the current.

Remember death

We avoid the topic of death. We pretend it won't happen to us—at least not for a long time. But really, death is the very thing that gives meaning to life. Death is a great teacher. It reminds us that, yes, our days here on this planet are numbered. It urges us to live to the maximum now. Knowing that you can die at any moment, why not live fully now? Live your last wishes now. Say yes to life now.

Forget about what is doable, likely or nice. Forget about someday. Be unreasonable. Be bold. Visualize something so big and exciting that

it scares you. Of course, the robotic mind will object once again. Left
to its own devices, your mind will offer evidence of why you are too
old, too young, too out of shape or too broke to realize your dreams.
Ignore that and try again. What would be out-of-this-world fantastic?

> *"We don't stop playing because we grow old; we grow old*
> *because we stop playing."*
> **GEORGE BERNARD SHAW**

It's never too late to try new things and discover something new. Be
bold and fearless. Reclaim your childhood passions. What did you love
to do as a kid? Try something if for no other reason than it appeals to
you. Sign up for that dance class you have thought about for years.
Get creative. Sing, color, sculpt, write. Creative expression makes you
more productive, happier, more successful. New experiences take
you out of the robot mind that thinks it already knows everything. Do
something you've never done before. Break your own rules. Being
playful, active and engaged with life puts you in the Now. Death
reminds us that beauty, love and joy are here now.

> *"One needs to be an adventurer, always ready to risk the*
> *known for the unknown. And once one has tasted the joys*
> *of freedom and fearlessness, one never repents because*
> *then one knows what it means to live at the optimum. Then*
> *one knows what it means to burn your life's torch from both*
> *ends together. And even a single moment of that intensity is*
> *more gratifying than the whole eternity of mediocre living."*
> **OSHO**

PART FOUR
CREATE THE NEW STORY

Create the New Story

Life is not about getting things done or finding a routine and sticking to it. Life is not about sameness. It's about being authentic to who you are at your innermost core. It's about adventure and joy and fulfilling your purpose—whatever that may be. It is about love and connection and learning and evolving. It is about living at a higher level of awareness. Full aliveness means going beyond your programs, conditioning and beliefs about what is possible. It is about being completely, 100%, unapologetically *you*.

> *"Be yourself. Everyone else is already taken."*
> **OSCAR WILDE**

Lasting peace and happiness don't come from the external world. Just as every snowflake is unique, so too is every leaf, every tree, every animal and every human being on this planet. That includes you. When you know who you are and why you are here, what other people do, say or think is largely irrelevant.

It's time to tell a new story. Set aside the wounds, the fear, the old programs and beliefs. Who are you without the old story of your previous relationships, past jobs or current bad habits? Who are you beyond your university degree, affiliations, roles, accolades, labels and circumstances?

> *"Our past is a story existing only in our minds. Look, analyze, understand and forgive. Then, as quickly as possible, chuck it."*
> **MARIANNE WILLIAMSON**

Let's lovingly chuck that old story now. You don't need it. You are not the same person anymore. Make a ceremony out of it where you honor and appreciate everything in your life as important, if for no other reason than it got you here. Then release the old story forever by shredding, burning or burying it.

Grab a pen and paper and write "My Amazing Life" across the top. Begin your new story from a clean slate, drawing from your imagination and your inner core, knowing that there are no limits. Imagine you've already left your body and Planet Earth. Tell the story from that expanded place. What was your life really about? How were you supported? What was important to you? What are the gifts you offered the world? *That* is the story to tell. Create a story you can get excited about. Include your exciting dream or desires as if you've already experienced all of it. Ignore the robotic mind that wants to know *how*. You don't need to know how it will happen. Write about your ideal job even if it doesn't seem to exist now.

You can reframe every seemingly negative thing that happened and tell it as if it were the most amazing thing ever. Because that is the truth. All of that stuff got you here. It's not about making things up or changing the events that occurred. It's about telling a new story around those events from a glass-half-full (or even better, fully full) perspective instead of from the glass-half-empty mode we're used to. Challenge yourself to list 20 amazing things that you did or experienced. If you really get into this, you'll discover, perhaps to your utter amazement, that the good stuff outweighs the seemingly bad or negative, by a lot.

In this new story, you unplugged the robot. You listen to your intuition and trust its guidance. You live from inspiration, following your heart. You are plugged into nature, grounded in your body and connected with people who truly value your unique expression. You love yourself.

You accept all your bits and pieces. You are awake, aware and centered. You go with the flow of the present moment.

Write about all that is amazing about your life right now. Take your time with this. Make it fun. Then read your new story before bed. Intend for your subconscious mind to work on the how while you sleep and to give you new ideas and inspiration during the day.

Start living your new story now. Take action. Practice your new beliefs. Engage the world with curiosity and wonder. Embrace the moment you are in. Give thanks in advance. Direct your thoughts as the conscious creator that you are.

NOW WHAT?

Unplug Your Robot, like all my books, is intentionally short. There is no fluff or fillers. In fact, you can read the entire book in one or two sittings. I hope you didn't. Reading it straight through is a sure sign that you skipped most of the suggested exercises and contemplations. Don't despair. You're not alone. Consider rereading the book, but this time experiment with each method to unplug your robot.

If you would like help with your daily practice of unplugging the robot and reconnecting to the real you, check out the companion playbook, available at http://UnplugYourRobotPlaybook.com.

Receive support in living your new story—and going beyond all stories—with personal coaching programs and transformational retreats. See the current offerings at www.KarinKiser.com.

NOTES

Although I can cite statistics, sources and internet sites for the things I mention, for this book I chose not to. As you might have experienced in researching any topic online, today's internet is ripe with censorship and fabrication. You can find what appears to be solid evidence for just about any statement or point of view no matter how ludicrous. Therefore, discerning what is true often comes down to two methods:

1. You know something is true when you have experienced it personally. For example, in *Chapter Ten: Connect with Nature*, I mention that we (Americans at least) spend more than 90% of our time indoors either in buildings or in automobiles. Calculate whether this is true for you in your own life.

2. Another method of knowing that doesn't require an internet search is your intuition, a feeling or knowingness in the core of your being that something is right.

I invite you to play with both methods as you read (or reread) this book.

ACKNOWLEDGEMENTS

I am grateful for all the perceived obstacles, routines, beliefs, bad habits, conditioning, triggers and rigid thinking in my own life that made writing this book a necessity—and allowed me to walk my talk on a deeper level.

ABOUT THE AUTHOR

KARIN KISER is the founder of Radical Simplicity™ and author of 10 books, including the international bestseller *Lighten Your Load*. She helps people simplify and detox their lives so they can live at a higher level with more time, energy, simplicity and ease. As a visionary and mentor, she inspires individuals around the world to greater health and happiness by teaching them to reduce the physical, mental and emotional toxins blocking their path.

She has worked with hundreds individually to live lighter on the planet, laugh more, breathe more and be more. *Unplug Your Robot* is the third book in the Dare to Be Aware™ series. Learn more about her work at www.KarinKiser.com.

OTHER BOOKS BY KARIN KISER

Lighten Your Load: 35 Surprisingly Simple Ways to Free Yourself from Stress, Toxins and Clutter

Free and Clear: 7 Steps to Declutter Your Home and Your Head

Your Inner Camino: Your Pocket Guide to Inspiration and Transformation Along the Camino de Santiago

After the Camino: Your Pocket Guide to Integrating the Camino de Santiago into Your Daily Life

---

Aligera tu carga: 35 estrategias sorprendentemente sencillas para liberarte del estrés, las toxinas y el desorden

Libérate del desorden: 7 pasos para despejar tu hogar y tu mente

El camino hacia tu interior: Tu guía de bolsillo para la inspiración y la transformación a través del Camino de Santiago

Después del camino: Tu guía de bolsillo para integrar el Camino de Santiago en tu vida diaria

Made in the USA
Monee, IL
19 September 2023